Strategy, Policy, and Review Department

Creating Policy Space in Low-Income Countries during the Recent Crises

Yongzheng Yang, Paolo Dudine, Eteri Kvintradze,
Pritha Mitra, Nkunde Mwase, and Sibabrata Das

INTERNATIONAL MONETARY FUND

Production: IMF Multimedia Services Division
Typesetting: Alicia Etchebarne-Bourdin

Cataloging-in-Publication Data

Creating policy space in low-income countries during the recent crises/Yongzheng Yang . . . [et al.].—Washington, D.C.: International Monetary Fund, 2009.

Includes bibliographical references.

ISBN 978-1-58906-930-5

1. Economic assistance—Developing countries. 2. International Monetary Fund—Developing countries. 3. Conditionality (International relations). 4. Monetary policy—Developing countries. 5. Fiscal policy—Developing countries. I. Yang, Yongzheng. II. International Monetary Fund. III. Title.

HC60.Y36 2009

Please send orders to:
International Monetary Fund, Publication Services
700 19th Street, NW, Washington, DC 20431, U.S.A.
Telephone: (202) 623-7430 Fax: (202) 623-7201
Internet: www.imfbookstore.org

Contents

Figures

Abbreviations and Acronyms

CSO	Civil Society Organization
DSA	Debt Sustainability Analysis
EFF	Extended Fund Facility
ESF	Exogenous Shocks Facility
FDI	Foreign Direct Investment
GDP	Gross Domestic Product
HAC	High-Access Component (of ESF)
HIPC	Heavily Indebted Poor Countries
IEO	Independent Evaluation Office (IMF)
LIC	Low-Income Country
MDG	Millennium Development Goal
MDRI	Multilateral Debt Relief Initiative
MONA	Monitoring of Fund Arrangements
PFM	Public Financial Management
PRGF	Poverty Reduction and Growth Facility
PRS	Poverty Reduction Strategy
PSI	Policy Support Instrument
RAC	Rapid-Access Component (of ESF)
SBA	Stand-By Arrangement
WEO	*World Economic Outlook*

Preface

Low-income countries have been hit hard by the sharp increases in world food and fuel prices in 2007–08 and subsequently by the global financial crisis and ensuing recession. The International Monetary Fund (IMF) has responded quickly to the need of its low-income country members to address the impact of these global shocks. It has substantially scaled up its financial assistance to low-income countries and revamped its concessional lending facilities to make them more flexible. Together with the ongoing reforms to streamline structural conditionality, these efforts have formed an important part of the IMF's strategy to help low-income countries address the fallout from the crises.

This Departmental Paper provides an initial empirical assessment of the outcome of these efforts and reforms. It examines the responsiveness of macroeconomic policies and structural conditionality in recent IMF-supported programs in a number of low-income countries. We hope the results of this exercise will help improve understanding of how IMF-supported programs in low-income countries have been adapted to the changing economic circumstances and which aspects of program design may need further improvement in the future.

Many people contributed to the undertaking of this exercise and to the production of this paper. Hugh Bredenkamp, Deputy Director of the Strategy, Policy, and Review Department of the IMF, and Catherine Pattillo, Advisor and Chief of the Low-Income Countries Strategy Unit of the Department, oversaw the exercise and provided invaluable guidance. The paper benefited enormously from data and comments provided by many staff, both within and outside the Strategy, Policy, and Review Department. Neri Gomes helped with administrative and editorial work, and Joanne Blake and her team helped turn the original paper into this Departmental Paper. We are grateful to all these colleagues.

Yongzheng Yang
Paolo Dudine
Eteri Kvintradze
Pritha Mitra
Nkunde Mwase
Sibabrata Das

CHAPTER

1 Overview

The IMF has been at the forefront in helping low-income countries (LICs) address the macroeconomic impact of the global food, fuel, and financial crises. LICs have been hard hit by massive increases in world food and fuel prices during 2007–08 and subsequently by the global financial crisis. In response, the Fund has dramatically stepped up its financial assistance to LICs, revised its conditionality framework, and revamped its concessional lending facilities. These developments are the culmination of an extended period of internal reform in response to a changing global environment. Some critics have nevertheless continued to express concern that Fund-supported programs may impose overly tight macroeconomic policies and burdensome structural conditionality.

The analysis in this paper finds that, in fact, the design of recent LIC programs has shown considerable flexibility, providing expanded policy space in the face of the crises:

- *Programs became progressively accommodating to the increasing world food and fuel prices in setting inflation objectives.* As food and fuel prices rose during 2007–08, inflation targets in programs were revised upward to accommodate the first-round effects of the rising world prices. As world prices fell sharply beginning in mid-2008, a gradual transition to single-digit inflation was programmed, leaving room for monetary policy to support economic activity during the global financial crisis.
- *Fiscal policy has accommodated larger deficits during the crises.* Most programs began to incorporate fiscal easing in 2007, with further relaxation of the fiscal stance in 2008 and 2009 in response to the world food and fuel price shocks and the global financial crisis. Close to two-thirds of the programs designed during 2007–09 increased the level of spending over time, while revenue declined. Increased donor support has helped meet part of the additional financing need, but many countries have resorted to domestic financing, and some have seen heightened risks to debt sustainability.

- *Recent programs have placed emphasis on strengthening social protection for the most vulnerable.* Most programs initiated in 2008–09 have envisaged higher social spending, with many also focusing on better targeting of social spending. However, countries will continue to face challenges in implementing their social spending plans due to capacity constraints. Further improvements are needed in targeting subsidies to the most needy.

- *Programs have accommodated widening current account deficits, financed partly by drawing on foreign reserves.* As world food and fuel prices rose during 2007, programs designed in that year began to target larger current account deficits in 2008 to ease the external account adjustment. As the global financial crisis hit, larger deficits continued to be accommodated by reserve drawdowns. Increases in external support, including a substantial scaling up of Fund assistance, have mitigated financing pressure.

- *Past successes in macroeconomic stabilization have created the needed space in many LICs for countercyclical responses during the crises.* Countries with lower debt risks—thanks to improved macroeconomic management and debt relief—have been well placed to adopt countercyclical responses to the crises in the fiscal and external accounts. Looking forward, it is critical that macroeconomic policies continue to safeguard stability while supporting short-term economic activity. As the impact of the global financial crises unwinds, countries need to reverse spending that was meant to be temporary to ensure medium-term debt sustainability.

The analysis also shows that structural conditionality has become more streamlined in recent years:

- *The number of conditions per program review has been declining since 2001–04.* The average number has fallen from nine conditions per review during 2001–04—the last period covered by the 2007 evaluation by the Independent Evaluation Office—to six in 2008–09. The number of "extreme" cases, programs with 15 or more conditions per review, dropped to zero during 2008–09.

- *Public sector resource management and accountability remain a key focus of structural conditionality.* This is by far the dominant category of conditionality. It falls clearly in the area of Fund specialization and is widely acknowledged, even by many Fund critics, as critical to achieving program goals in LICs.

- *Structural conditionality has responded to the increasing need to mitigate pressures on public finances during the twin global crises.* Programs initiated in 2008–09 included more conditions on fiscal policy measures in the face of declining revenue and mounting spending needs to support economic activity and protect the poor.

- *As the number of conditions has declined, the implementation rate has improved.* Since 2001–04, the proportion of conditions met per review has risen by 15 percent, to 86 percent. This should bode well for country ownership of programs as greater parsimony in conditionality enables governments to concentrate their scarce administrative resources on priority reforms.

Looking ahead, policies will need to remain adaptive to the evolving circumstances. Despite encouraging signs of a rebounding global economy, the timing and strength of economic recovery in LICs remain uncertain. Meanwhile, LICs continue to face large financing needs, not only for economic stabilization in the short run, but also for restoring and sustaining strong growth over the long run. These challenges will continue to test the flexibility of the Fund in devising appropriate macroeconomic policies and critical structural reforms in helping LICs achieve their development goals.

CHAPTER

2 Background

The IMF has been at the forefront in helping low-income countries (LICs) address the macroeconomic impact of the global food, fuel, and financial crises. LICs were hard hit by massive increases in food and fuel prices during 2007–08, followed closely by a wave of shocks associated with the global financial crisis. In response, the Fund has dramatically increased its financial assistance to LICs, with higher access limits, a more flexible framework for structural conditionality, and revamped lending facilities. At the same time, the Fund has stepped up its policy advice and technical assistance to its LIC members to address their capacity constraints. These efforts have intensified a process of reform within the Fund aimed at increasing the institution's flexibility in adapting to a changing global environment, including the increasing diversity of economic challenges in LICs.

The scaling up of Fund resources for assisting LICs has been unprecedented. Under a new package of measures approved by the IMF's Executive Board on July 29, 2009, the Fund will boost its concessional lending capacity to about US$17 billion through 2014, including up to US$8 billion over the next two years, a sharp increase over the US$1.6 billion lending commitments in 2008. The new package also provides for zero interest payments through end-2011 on new and outstanding concessional loans, as well as permanently higher concessionality of Fund financial support thereafter. In addition, under the US$250 billion general allocation of Special Drawing Rights that became effective on August 28, 2009, LICs have received more than US$18 billion to bolster their foreign exchange reserves and thereby ease their financing constraints.

The increased resources will be channeled through a new architecture of lending facilities for LICs. The new architecture, also part of the July package, represents a comprehensive redesign of the Fund's lending toolkit and is aimed at making Fund lending more flexible and tailored to varying needs of LICs.[1] While preserving the recent doubling of loan access limits and streamlined conditionality requirements, the revamped facilities will close gaps in the previous lending framework and streamline existing instruments to provide more effective support to LICs, especially for short-term, precautionary, and emergency needs. Moreover, the revamped facilities will reinforce the links between Fund-supported programs and country poverty reduction strategies (PRS). In the same spirit, the Executive Board recently approved a more flexible approach to setting debt limits in Fund-supported programs to better reflect the considerable diversity among LICs, in terms of their debt vulnerabilities and macroeconomic and public financial management (PFM) capacity.

These recent reforms were initiated against the backdrop of past criticisms of the Fund's engagement with LICs. There has long been concern about the effects of macroeconomic policy design on poverty reduction and growth and about the effectiveness of structural conditionality in Fund-supported programs. The Fund's responses to the impact of the recent global crises have also been subject to close scrutiny by key stakeholders, especially after the G-20 gave the Fund a central role in dealing with the global financial crisis. Although the Fund has highlighted its increased responsiveness to the needs of its member countries, many civil society organizations (CSOs) have expressed concern that the Fund continues to prescribe macroeconomic policies that are too tight and impose structural conditionality that is burdensome and ineffective.[2]

Against that background, this paper offers an empirical analysis of the Fund's flexibility in the face of the "twin crises." It does not purport to provide a comprehensive review of recent LIC programs. Rather, its intention is to shed light on two key questions that have been raised: namely, have Fund-supported programs provided the macroeconomic policy space that LICs needed to confront the recent crises; and has the Fund lived up to its rhetoric in streamlining and focusing structural conditionality in recent years?[3]

The rest of the paper is organized as follows. Chapter 3 provides an overview of the key principles governing program design in LICs and an empirical analysis of macroeconomic policy design in Fund-supported programs

[1]See IMF (2009a). Recent reforms of the Fund's lending facilities began with a modification of the Exogenous Shocks Facility (ESF) in September 2008 to address the impact of the increases in global food and fuel prices in 2008. The ESF was made faster to access, easier to use, and capable of providing more financing. At the time this report was prepared the July 2009 package was expected to become effective after the required consents of contributors to the Poverty Reduction and Growth Facility (PRGF)-ESF Trust are received.

[2]See Eurodad (2009) and Third World Network (2009).

[3]This is therefore a more limited exercise than the much broader assessment of recent IMF-supported programs in emerging market countries (IMF, 2009b).

initiated immediately before and during the crises. Chapter 4 outlines the evolution of the Fund's policy on structural conditionality since the early 2000s and examines recent practice, looking both at the extent and the focus of conditionality. Chapter 5 concludes.

CHAPTER

3 Responsiveness in Macroeconomic Policy Design

Addressing Shocks: The Strategic Approach

IMF-supported programs are aimed at resolving balance of payments problems encountered by its member countries. Restoring external balance is essential to achieving macroeconomic stability, which in turn is a precondition for sustained economic growth and poverty reduction.[4] Balance of payments problems often stem from external shocks, but they also often result from overly expansionary fiscal and/or monetary policies, and/or a misaligned exchange rate. The resolution of balance of payments problems therefore often requires policy adjustment to bring the economy back on a sustainable path, together with external financing to smooth the adjustment process.

It is in this context that the IMF has often been criticized for imposing overly tight macroeconomic policies to bring about needed adjustment. Concerns have centered on the impact of adjustment on public spending (including on government wage bills), restrictive monetary policy, and (implicitly, at least) insufficient financing.[5] In the past, Fund-supported programs in some countries sought to restrain government wage bills that could pose a threat to government finances and divert scarce resources away from critical spending on poverty reduction and growth. Critics have argued that this often had adverse consequences for hiring workers in social sectors, such as health and education.

The Fund's concessional lending policies have evolved over the years in part to address such concerns. Programs supported by the Poverty Reduction and

---

[4]See Ghosh and others (2005) for a recent examination of the design of IMF-supported programs.

[5]In programs that the Fund supports, it aims to play a catalytic role to mobilize donor support to meet required external financing. For this reason, the Fund typically provides a portion of total financing required. Moreover, the Fund has an obligation to protect its financial resources and to ensure their revolving use to meet continuous financing demand by its members.

Growth Facility (PRGF), the Fund's main lending facility for LICs over the past decade, are anchored by country-owned PRS (IMF and World Bank, 1999a, 1999b). PRGF-supported programs have put increased emphasis on ensuring higher budgetary allocations for poverty-reducing spending and more flexible fiscal frameworks to accommodate higher aid flows (IMF, 2002a, 2005a). Some of the most controversial aspects of program design, such as ceilings on public sector wage bills, have virtually disappeared. Today, none of the 37 Fund-supported programs in LICs contains a wage bill ceiling as a performance criterion, and only three have indicative targets—a nonbinding condition—on the wage bill.

The twin global crises during 2008–09 have provided an unparalleled test of the Fund's capability to adapt macroeconomic policy design to a changing economic environment. Never before have LICs experienced such large and diverse shocks in a short space of two years. As world prices for food and fuel soared from 2007 to mid-2008, many LICs saw their inflation rising, budget outlays increasing and current account deficits mounting. The subsequent decline in commodity prices and the global financial crisis reduced inflation pressures, but they put further strain on many LICs' budgets and balance of payments as revenue dwindled with slowing growth, export demand and remittances fell, and capital flows reversed (see Box 3.1). To deal with these challenges, macroeconomic policy design needed to strike the right balance between adjustment and accommodation. Although it is critical to preserve the hard-won macroeconomic stability gains by avoiding high inflation and ensuring sustainable fiscal and external debt in the medium term, macroeconomic policies should, to the greatest extent possible, sustain short-term economic activity and protect the poor by accommodating increased financing needs.

How accommodating macroeconomic policies can be depends critically on each country's starting conditions. On the whole, LICs went into the storms of the twin crises in a much stronger position than ever before.[6] Over the past decade, economic growth had picked up pace, and inflation had been brought down to single digits (Figure 3.1). Government finances were strengthened considerably, with improved fiscal balances and sharply lower levels of public debt, thanks to better economic management as well as debt relief. Foreign reserves in LICs had increased substantially, providing many countries with a buffer against external shocks. These improvements, of course, mask considerable variations across countries. Right before the food

[6]IMF (2009c) shows that over the past two decades, countries with a long-term program engagement with the Fund have on average achieved a more pronounced increase in long-term growth and more sizable reductions in inflation, debt, and current account and fiscal deficits than countries with little or no program engagement.

Box 3.1. The Impact of the Global Food, Fuel, and Financial Crises on LICs

The food and fuel price crisis had a significant impact on LICs. A worldwide commodity price rise picked up pace in 2007 and climaxed in mid-2008. Food prices rose by 45 percent from end-2006, and many prices reached record highs in current U.S. dollar terms—including those for crude oil, tin, nickel, soybeans, corn and wheat. External balances of net commodity importers deteriorated considerably, and headline inflation increased sharply in many LICs, leading to price-related riots in some countries. Although external balances of net commodity exporters improved, domestic inflation in these countries also rose rapidly. Most LICs passed on, at least partially, world price increases to domestic prices, which often led to the need to protect the most vulnerable segments of the population. For countries that did not pass on world prices, increased budget outlays became necessary to keep domestic prices low. Many Fund-supported programs in 2007 and 2008 were designed against this background.

While LICs were still dealing with the consequences of the food and fuel crisis, they were hit by the global financial crisis in late 2008. As the world economy went into recession, demand for LIC exports fell sharply. Commodity exporters have been hit especially hard by the collapse of world prices. The World Trade Organization reported that world trade contracted by a third during the first half of 2009 compared with the same period in 2008. At the same time, remittance flows are slowing and expected to decline for most countries in 2009. The World Bank projects that remittances to developing countries are likely to fall by 7–10 percent in 2009 (Ratha, Mohapatra, and Silwal, 2009). Foreign direct investment (FDI) and other capital inflows are also contracting. Those LICs that had begun to access international financial markets have seen this access come virtually to an end. These adverse developments have led to a large external financing need in many LICs (IMF, 2009e). The global financial crisis has also worsened the budgetary position of many LIC governments. While the need for spending is increasing to protect the poor and to stimulate growth, revenue collections are either slowing or declining as economic activity slows and commodity prices fall. Potential declines in donor support may put further pressure on the budget in many LICs.

and fuel price crisis, more than a third of LICs faced high risks of debt distress (based on debt sustainability analyses [DSAs] jointly undertaken by the World Bank and the IMF). Some LICs continued to exhibit high inflation, large fiscal deficits and low reserves.

Against this background, the IMF has advised different strategies, according to the nature of the shocks and initial country conditions. Policy advice to LICs affected by food and fuel price shocks was to allow world prices to pass through to domestic markets and accommodate the first-round effects of the shocks by raising inflation targets. Where fiscal and external debt sustainability was not at risk, countries were advised to allow larger fiscal and current account deficits. In this context, the Fund also encouraged measures

Figure 3.1. Selected Macroeconomic Indicators: 1995–2008[1]

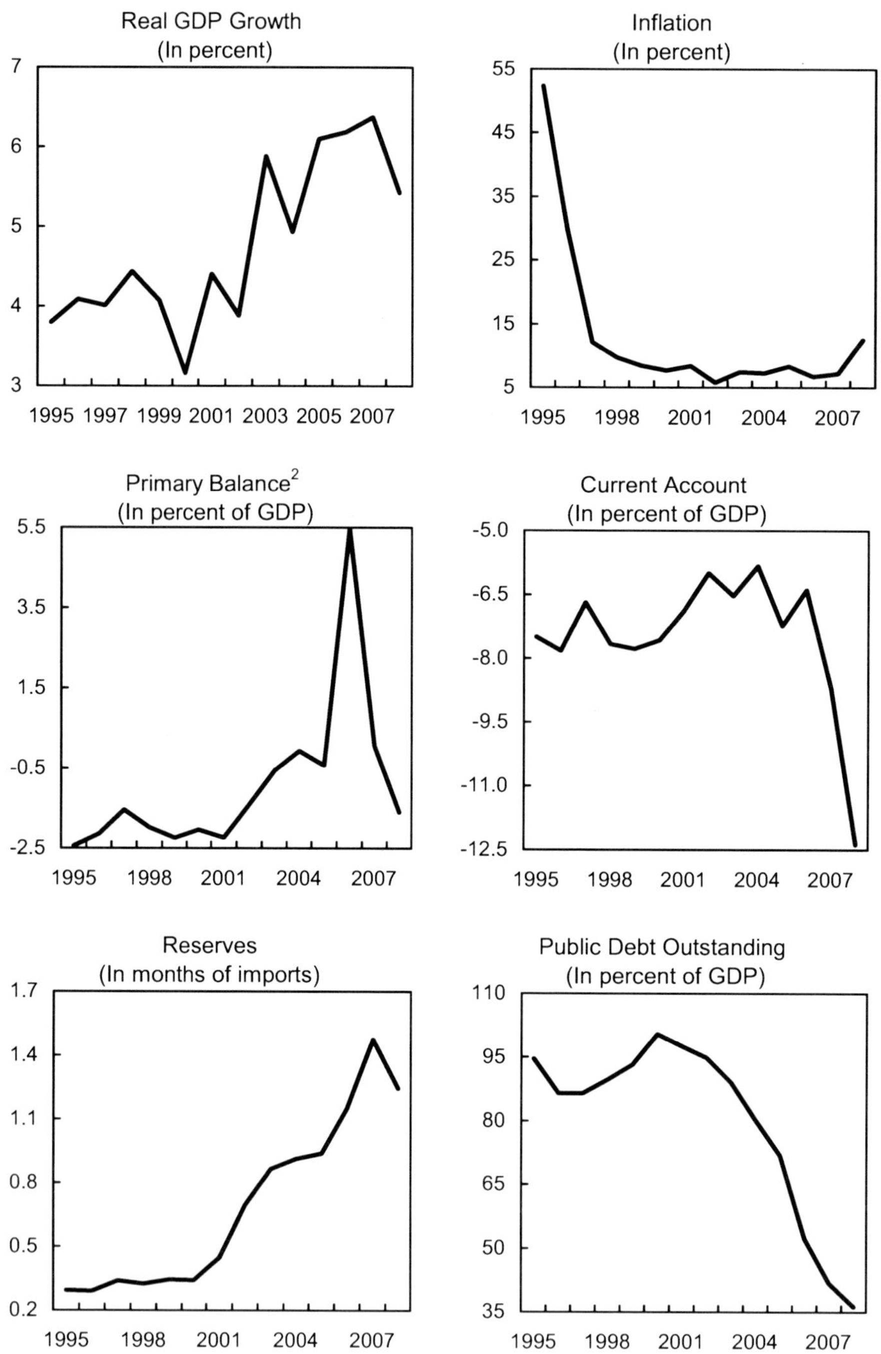

Sources: WEO database; and authors' estimates.

[1]Data cover 37 program LICs.

[2]2006 data for primary balance reflect the effect of debt relief under the Multilateral Debt Relief Initiative (MDRI).

to mitigate the impact of the price increases on the poor, including through targeted subsidies, while minimizing disincentives for positive long-run supply responses. Once the global financial crisis and recession hit, the Fund's advice to its members—advanced economies, emerging market countries, and LICs alike—emphasized the need to sustain short-term economic activity to the extent possible while maintaining medium-term debt sustainability. In countries with strong debt positions, the Fund has seen scope to accommodate the cyclical fiscal deterioration and, when financing is available, to increase spending to cushion the impact of the crisis on the economy.[7] In LICs with highly vulnerable debt and binding fiscal constraints, the Fund has advised the reprioritization of resources needed to protect social and other core spending. In many LICs, the ability to offset adverse shocks through spending hinges on the level of donor support, the prospects for which are uncertain following a welcome increase in 2008.

The Fund has already begun developing advice on exit strategies to ensure a smooth transition from crisis response to a focus on medium-term growth and debt sustainability. Policies for the recovery phase, like those for the initial shocks, cannot be one-size-fits-all. For countries where growth is expected to remain weak for some time and debt sustainability is not a major concern, there is room to withdraw stimulus slowly to avoid a prolonged economic downturn, while those facing severe debt vulnerabilities may need to tighten macroeconomic policies more quickly. Continued structural reforms are important to raise growth potential and reduce debt vulnerabilities in both groups of countries. Further improvements in revenue administration, public financial management and debt management are needed to mobilize more resources and use them more efficiently.

Applying the Strategy: Policy Easing in Response to the Crises

How have these policy principles translated into practice? Almost a year into the global recession, we can offer a preliminary assessment. The analysis in this section looks at how targets for key macroeconomic variables evolved during 2007–09 in LICs that had a continuous program engagement with the Fund over that period.[8]

[7]See Berg and others (2009).

[8]The results reported are for countries with continuous PRGF-supported programs (see Box 3.2). Annex I provides an analysis for a broader sample, including LICs supported under other Fund facilities, and finds similar results. The findings of this section are further corroborated by an analysis including noncontinuous PRGF program engagement over the same period (not reported here).

Figure 3.2. Key Program Variables[1]

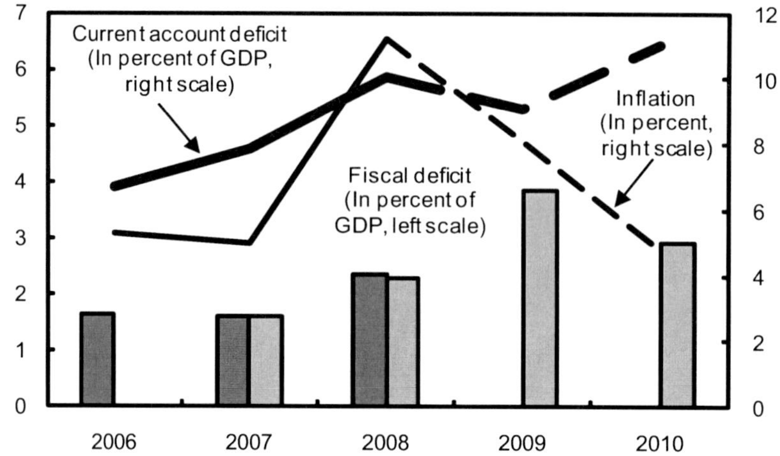

Source: Authors' estimates based on IMF staff reports.
[1]Solid lines and darker bars represent actuals, while dashed lines and lighter bars refer to projections. All projections for 2009 and 2010 are taken from 2009 program documents. For fiscal deficits, projections for 2007 and 2008 are taken from program documents for 2007 and 2008, respectively.

The evidence suggests considerable adaptation in program design in response to the shocks incurred during the twin crises. In the course of 2007 and 2008, programs in LICs affected by food and fuel price shocks accommodated higher inflation and current account deficits, and began to provide for larger fiscal deficits, at least where fiscal and external debt sustainability was not at risk (Figure 3.2). In that period, the Fund also encouraged measures to mitigate the impact of the price increases on the poor, including through targeted subsidies.[9] During the global financial crisis of 2008–09, program design varied with initial macroeconomic conditions, but generally it reflected a decline in inflation due to receding food and fuel prices, and allowed automatic stabilizers to work (essentially on the revenue side), while accommodating higher spending, in many cases, together with larger fiscal and current account deficits. Box 3.3 describes how the design of programs in the Kyrgyz Republic and Zambia was adapted over time in response to the successive shocks.

[9]See IMF (2009d).

Box 3.2. Defining the Data

The analysis in this section focuses on countries that had a continuous program engagement with the Fund under the PRGF during January 2007–June 2009.[1] The rationale for this choice is that:

- PRGF-supported programs accounted for the bulk of Fund-supported programs in LICs over that period.
- By design, macroeconomic adjustment under a PRGF-supported program takes place over a three-year period. This allows the Fund to assess whether and how flexibly programs reflect changes in the economic environment.
- Continuous program engagement during the period 2007–09 ensures that data reflect changes in program design for a relatively homogeneous group of countries.

A country is included in the dataset if it had at least one PRGF request or review in each of the years 2007, 2008, and 2009 (up to June). To maximize the sample size, three countries that had a PRGF-supported program in both 2007 and 2008 and subsequently replaced it with a High-Access Component (HAC) of the Exogenous Shocks Facility (ESF) in 2009 are also included. In cases where a country did not have a review in 2008, it is still included if it had a review in 2009 under the same program that the country had in 2007. For programs that had multiple reviews in a year, averages across reviews are used. Data for each country come from program documents discussed by the Executive Board of the IMF.[2]

By comparing program design for the same group of countries in successive years, and under the same program or under successor programs, it is possible to assess how key macroeconomic policy parameters evolved as country circumstances changed.

[1] The following countries are included in the dataset: Afghanistan, Albania, Benin, Burkina Faso, Burundi, Cameroon, the Central African Republic, The Gambia, Grenada, Haiti, the Kyrgyz Republic, Malawi, Mali, Niger, Rwanda, Sierra Leone, and Zambia. São Tomé and Príncipe was not included because its high program variable ratios relative to GDP place it as an outlier in most of the analysis.

[2] For a more detailed explanation of the dataset, see Berndt and others (2008).

PRGF-supported programs began to factor in the impact of the twin crises on growth starting in 2008. Programs designed in 2007 did not anticipate an economic downturn in the short run: on average, these programs were projecting growth of about 5.7 percent in 2007 and about 6.3 percent in 2008, in line with actual growth in 2006 (Figure 3.3).[10] These projections

[10] The panels in Figure 3.3 show for some key macroeconomic variables the averages across countries and across program reviews and requests made in different years. In each panel, the three lines refer to programs that were designed (that is, either requested or reviewed) in 2007 (solid black line), 2008 (light gray line), and 2009 (dark gray line), respectively. The leftmost point of each line (square) shows the average the year before programs were designed; the central point (triangle) shows the average for the same year programs were designed; and the rightmost point (circle) shows the average projection for the year ahead.

Box 3.3. Macroeconomic Policy Responses to the Crises in the Kyrgyz Republic and Zambia

The Kyrgyz Republic

This country was one of the first to take advantage of the revamped ESF and received US$100 million under the ESF-HAC in December 2008. The program under the ESF was aimed at addressing the consequences of higher world food and fuel prices and a regional slowdown (particularly in Russia and Kazakhstan, which are the main sources of remittances and trade) as a result of the global financial crisis. At the time of the request for financial assistance under the ESF, the Kyrgyz Republic was experiencing a sharp slowdown in growth, rising inflation, a widening current account deficit and increasing spending pressures. Against this background, the program sought to reduce inflation to close to 10 percent by end-2009, while sustaining and accelerating growth, and protecting the poor.

The initial program design was more accommodating than the preceding PRGF-supported program for which the sixth (and last) review was completed in May 2008. The 2008 inflation target under the ESF program was higher in view of the larger impact of the world food and fuel price increases than anticipated at the time of the sixth review. The primary fiscal deficit was programmed to widen in 2009–10 despite an unexpected improvement in 2008, and the external current account deficit was projected to increase substantially during 2008–10. At the time of the first review of the ESF program in May 2009, program targets were further relaxed in response to a worsening economic outlook. Most notably, despite significantly lower expected revenue, expenditures were programmed to increase compared to the initial program.

The Kyrgyz Republic: Selected Economic Indicators under the ESF-Supported Program

	2007	2008	2009	2010
Real GDP growth (percent)	8.5	7.6	0.9	2.9
Consumer price index (average, percent)	10.2	24.5	12.4	8.6
Primary balance excl. grants (percent of GDP)	–1.9	–1.1	–6.7	–6.1
Revenue (percent of GDP)	22.6	23.3	19.2	19.7
Expenditure (percent of GDP)	31.0	29.6	31.3	30.9
Social Fund Expenditure (percent of GDP)	5.3	5.1	5.7	6.0
Current account balance, excl. transfers (percent of GDP)	–1.0	–7.3	–10.2	–9.2
Gross reserves (months of imports)	3.0	3.6	3.9	3.5

Source: *The Kyrgyz Republic—Staff Report for the 2009 Article IV Consultation and First Review Under the 18-Month Arrangement Under the Exogenous Shocks Facility*, IMF Country Report No. 09/209, July 2009.

A salient feature of program design in the Kyrgyz Republic is the increase in social spending to mitigate the effects of the global financial crisis on the poor. Budget allocations to the Unified Monthly Benefit—a social assistance program that targets poor households with children—are programmed to increase over the period 2009–11. Strong growth, successful fiscal consolidation and improved revenue administration in the recent past have enabled the government to beef up social spending when it is most needed. This is made possible also by significant donor support (equivalent to 9 percent of GDP) from Russia, along with debt relief.

There are early signs that the policy easing has helped mitigate the impact of the crises. In particular, growth is better than would have been expected given the sharp retrenchments in Russia and Kazakhstan. Increased government spending on infrastructure and social protection has helped bolster domestic demand. Inflation has fallen sharply, to about 3 percent in August 2009, with a positive impact on external competitiveness and real household income and spending.

Box 3.3 *(concluded)*

Zambia

Zambia's current program is supported by a low-access three-year arrangement under the PRGF approved in May 2008, after the successful completion of a PRGF-supported program in September 2007. The current program aims to maintain macroeconomic stability and debt sustainability, while increasing fiscal space for investment in infrastructure, energy and human resources. To meet these objectives, the initial program was designed to reduce inflation significantly but, in accommodating the impact of higher world food and fuel prices, at a much slower pace than envisaged in the final review of the previous program. The program also projected some increase in the primary fiscal balance (excluding grants). The external current account was programmed to improve after 2008, and international reserve coverage was set to increase.

Macroeconomic policies were adjusted significantly at the time of the combined first and second reviews in April 2009. Financial assistance under the PRGF was augmented from 10 percent of quota to 45 percent. Given Zambia's relatively low level of public debt, fiscal policy was loosened for 2009–10. Monetary policy was eased toward the end of 2008 to accommodate the effects of higher world food and fuel prices, with the inflation target adjusted upward from the original program. The precipitous fall in the prices of copper and cobalt is expected to lead to a further widening of the current account deficit in 2009 after a larger than expected deficit in 2008. Revenue was also expected to fall in 2009, but expenditure was programmed to continue to increase. At the same time, the target for reserve accumulation was reduced from 4.7 months of imports in 2009 in the original program to just 3.1 months. Overall, the program's design has been adapted considerably to address the fallout from the global crises while trying to maintain external stability in the face of an exceptionally large terms-of-trade shock.

Recent data show that the adjustment of macroeconomic policies beginning in April 2009 has helped alleviate the impact of the crisis by providing the resources needed to help finance increased infrastructure and social spending. The increase in spending has helped to boost domestic demand and growth, and is critical to achieving Zambia's poverty reduction and economic diversification goals. Copper prices have also more than doubled since the start of the year, and contributed to the strengthened economic growth and balance of payments outlook. At the same time, inflation pressure is expected to ease, reflecting the recent appreciation of the kwacha and a bumper harvest.

Zambia: Selected Economic Indicators under the PRGF-Supported Program

	2007	2008	2009	2010
Real GDP growth (percent)	6.3	6.0	4.0	4.5
Consumer price index (average, percent)	10.7	12.4	12.5	8.3
Primary balance excl. grants (percent of GDP)	–3.1	–3.8	–5.8	–4.4
Revenue (percent of GDP)	18.7	19.0	17.7	17.9
Expenditure (percent of GDP)	23.5	24.6	25.3	24.0
Current account balance, excl. transfers (percent of GDP)	–9.3	–9.6	–12.1	–10.9
Official transfers (percent of GDP)	4.6	3.9	5.0	4.4
Gross reserves (months of imports)	2.5	2.1	3.1	3.1

Source: *Zambia—First and Second Review Under the Three-Year Arrangement Under the Poverty Reduction and Growth Facility, and Request for Waiver for Performance Criteria and Augmentation of Access*, IMF Country Report No. 09/188, June 2009.

Figure 3.3. Real GDP Growth and Inflation
(In percent)

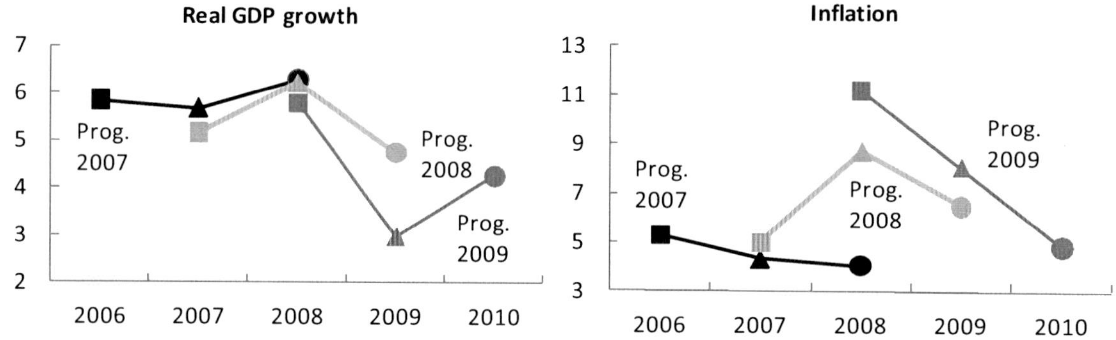

Source: Authors' estimates based on IMF staff reports.
■: Actual ▲: Projection for the year of program design ●: Program projection for the following year.

turned out to be broadly accurate. In 2008, however, programs began to incorporate expectations of an economic downturn for the following year: projected growth for 2009 was lowered by more than 1.5 percentage points. As programs were revised in 2009, projections for the current year were reduced even further, by as much as about 3 percentage points relative to 2008, followed by a moderate recovery in 2010.

Similarly, program design has been responsive to the inflation outlook as the global environment changed. Programs designed in 2007 aimed, on average, for declining inflation in both 2007 and 2008 (Figure 3.3). As the impact of the rising global food and fuel prices intensified in the first half of 2008, however, programs were adapted to accommodate much higher inflation targets for that year. When commodity prices went into reverse in the second half of 2008 and economic activity weakened, programs projected a decline in inflation for 2009. With declining money demand associated with slower growth, monetary policy was adjusted to provide for a gradual transition to a low inflation environment (Figure 3.4).

Most programs have been accommodating larger fiscal deficits since the beginning of the food and fuel crisis. About three-quarters of the programs were able to ease the fiscal stance in 2008–09. On average, targets set in 2007 already envisaged increased fiscal deficits for 2008 (Figure 3.5). In the course of 2008, programs were modified to create room for further fiscal easing in 2009, and deficit targets have been substantially scaled up again this year, in the wake of the crisis. Some partial adjustment is currently envisaged for 2010, in line with the expected pickup in economic growth.

Figure 3.4. Annual Growth in Broad Money
(In percent)

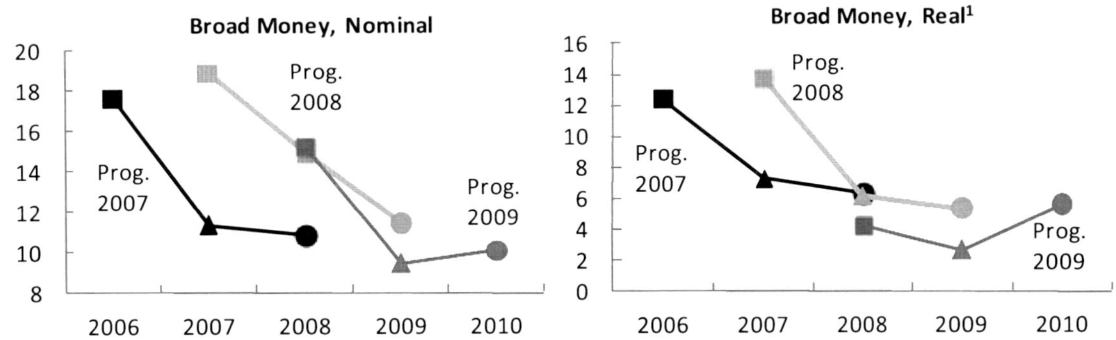

Source: Authors' estimates based on IMF staff reports.
■: Actual ▲: Projection for the year of program design ●: Program projection for the following year.
[1]Deflated by the consumer price index.

Figure 3.5. Fiscal Deficit, Including Grants
(In percent of GDP)

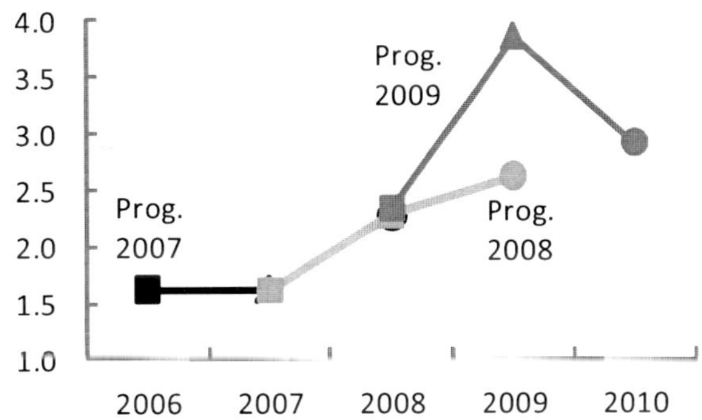

Source: Authors' estimates based on IMF staff reports.
■: Actual ▲: Projection for the year of program design ●: Program projection for the following year.

The programmed fiscal easing has typically involved letting automatic stabilizers work (at least on the revenue side), but with some margin also for spending increases.[11] Reflecting expectations of lower growth, revenue projections were broadly flat in 2008 programs and declining in 2009 programs (Figure 3.6). But in close to two-thirds of the programs, fiscal

[11]Automatic stabilizers are virtually nonexistent on the expenditure side in LICs owing to, among other things, their underdeveloped social protection systems. A well-developed system allows an automatic increase in spending in response to an economic downturn (for example, in the form of higher unemployment benefits).

Figure 3.6. Revenues, Net of Grants
(In percent of GDP)

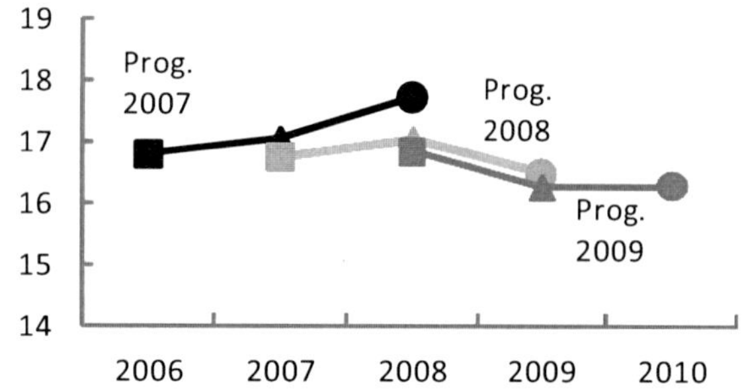

Figure 3.7. Total Spending
(In percent of GDP)

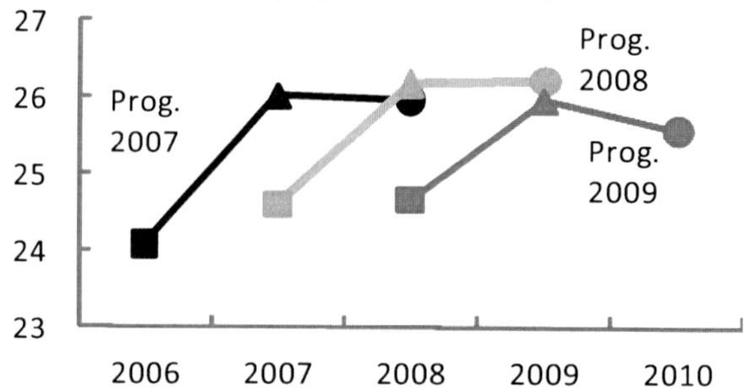

Source: Authors' estimates based on IMF staff reports.
■: Actual ▲: Projection for the year of program design ●: Program projection for the following year.

targets have been set to accommodate significant increases in government spending 1–2 years ahead, despite the bleaker revenue outlook. This "spending room" has been preserved each year even though, in 2007 and 2008, actual spending fell well short of target, most likely as a result of capacity constraints in implementing donor-supported spending. On average, total spending was programmed to increase by close to 2 percent of GDP over the period 2006–09 (Figure 3.7). In real terms, this translates into an average annual increase of almost 7.5 percent through 2009. Growth in real spending is expected to slow to about 3 percent in 2010, as the economic recovery begins and fiscal adjustment kicks in.

The scope for countercyclical fiscal policy varied in part according to debt sustainability constraints. In countries that were considered to have high debt risks, programs in 2008 targeted stable fiscal deficits broadly in line with the 2006–07 outturns. By contrast, programs in countries with low or moderate debt vulnerabilities accommodated increasing deficits for both 2007 and 2008 (Figure 3.8).[12] Since the beginning of this year, however, in response to the intensifying impact of the global financial crisis, programs in both groups of countries have generally targeted larger deficits in 2009, with some retrenchment in 2010. A noticeable difference is that, by next year, countries with high debt risk will broadly return to their (relatively high) deficit levels prevailing in 2006, whereas countries with low and moderate debt risk are expected to be running significantly larger deficits than they were before the crises. This highlights the importance of the stabilization gains of the past in creating needed fiscal space for countercyclical responses during the crises.

[12]The classification of the program countries according to their debt vulnerabilities is based on the joint assessments of the World Bank and IMF in their latest country DSAs.

Figure 3.8. Fiscal Deficit by Level of Debt Distress Risks
(In percent of GDP)

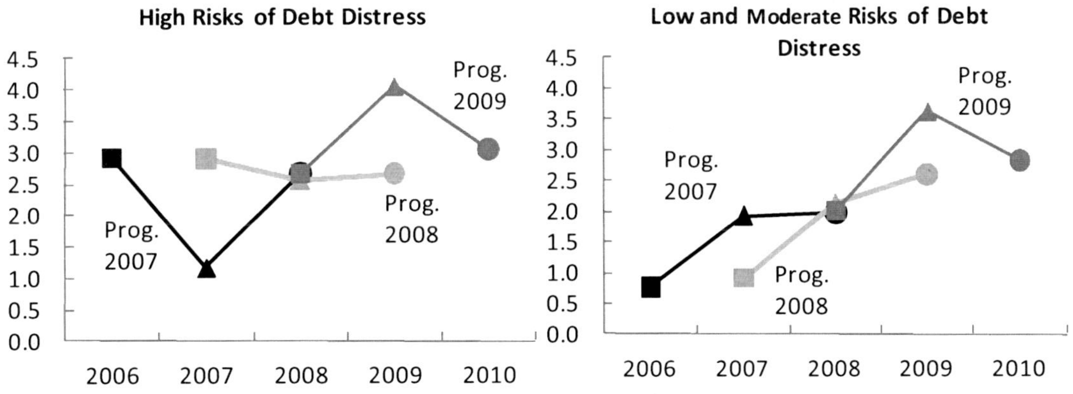

Source: Authors' estimates based on IMF staff reports.
■: Actual ▲: Projection for the year of program design ●: Program projection for the following year.

Increased donor support has helped finance part of the higher fiscal deficits, but many countries have resorted to additional domestic financing. On average, net external budget financing increased by about 0.25 percent of GDP in 2008, and has been projected to increase by about 0.75 percent of GDP in 2009. However, there is considerable uncertainty over the outcome for 2009 because projections of aid disbursements have tended to be overly optimistic in the past. Domestic financing expanded by about 1.5 percent of GDP in 2007–08 and is projected to increase by another 0.5 percent of GDP in 2009.[13] Based on a survey of a larger sample of LICs than covered in this analysis, the increase in domestic financing in 2009 is projected to be six times as large as the increase in external financing.[14] As the impact of the global financial crisis unwinds and local cyclical conditions normalize, the sharp increase in domestic financing may need to be reversed.

The twin crises have so far moderately increased debt vulnerabilities for LICs as a whole. However, only a small number of countries are at risk of moving into a higher vulnerability category as a result of the crises, and the outlook for these and other affected countries will depend critically on the future response of donors in providing additional highly concessional support, as well as on appropriately phased policy adjustment in the countries themselves.[15]

[13]Domestic financing here includes domestic borrowing and other sources, such as privatization receipts.

[14]See IMF (2009e).

[15]See IMF (2009e) for an analysis of debt vulnerabilities in a larger set of LICs.

Figure 3.9. Average Social Spending for Selected Countries[1]

(In percent of GDP)

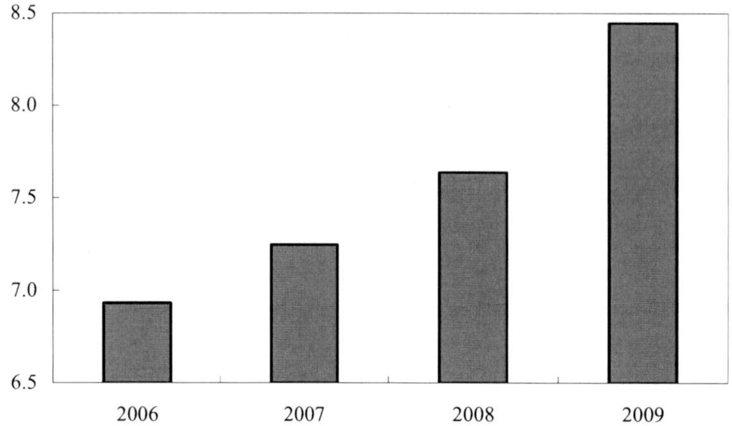

Sources: Country authorities; and authors' estimates.

[1] Includes Côte d'Ivoire, Djibouti, Georgia, Niger, Togo, Mozambique, Rwanda, and Senegal. The 2009 number is a projection.

The Social Dimension

Programs have placed considerable emphasis on strengthening social protection for the most vulnerable.[16] Out of the 19 programs initiated in 2008–09, 16 have budgeted higher social spending for 2009 (see Annex 3 for country details).[17] For eight countries that have reported a consistent data series over time, average social spending increased by 0.4 percent of GDP in 2008 and has been programmed to increase by 0.8 percent of GDP in 2009 (Figure 3.9).

These increases were achieved and planned mainly on account of expanding existing social benefits programs (the case of the Kyrgyz Republic, described in Box 3.3, is a good illustration of this). Given constraints on administrative capacity, many LICs will face challenges in carrying out their social spending plans for 2009. Nevertheless, it is encouraging that programs have given due recognition to the social stress created by the crises in LICs and thus have allowed room for additional social spending at a time when competing demand for public resources has been rising.

[16]The analysis of social spending here relies on a different set of data for the 19 countries that initiated a program (of any type) in 2008–09. The definition of social spending varies across countries.

[17]These include 15 countries for which social spending is expected to increase in real terms (IMF, 2009e, paragraph 43, page 20) and one country that, based on qualitative reports, is also expected to increase social spending.

Box 3.4. Improving Targeting of Social Spending

LICs with Fund-supported programs have applied various approaches to helping their poorest citizens, in the absence of well-developed social protection systems. Although many of these approaches may be less than ideal, they often constitute practical solutions to the pressing problems facing LIC governments. Fund-supported programs have supported countries' efforts in finding such practical solutions:

- *Improving existing systems and programs.* Some LICs see potential to make their current systems and programs more effective in delivering social benefits. Senegal and Burkina Faso, for example, have switched away from temporary food price measures that were not well targeted to the poor. Many countries have sought assistance from the World Bank and the regional development banks in evaluating existing systems and programs with a view to improving targeting (e.g., Djibouti, Ghana, Mali, Mongolia, and Pakistan).
- *Subsidies and cash transfers.* Some countries have used subsidies for specific activities or social groups to increase social support. Direct distribution of food, seeds and fertilizers to the needy has been an important way of improving targeting of social benefits in some countries (e.g., Burundi and Mali), and provision of free school uniforms and free textbooks (e.g., Ghana) has also been common. Temporary removal of import duties on essential food and energy products has also been used (e.g., Mali). Some other countries are focusing on the development of social services, such as in health, education and public utilities (e.g., São Tomé and Príncipe and Zambia). In Pakistan, the government provided direct cash transfers to the poor.
- *Focus on improving social indicators.* In HIPC countries, considerable attention has been paid to the monitoring of pro-poor spending and progress on social indicators (e.g., Republic of the Congo, Côte d'Ivoire, Djibouti, Liberia, Mali, Niger, Togo, and São Tomé and Príncipe). Fund-supported programs have provided a vehicle to monitor pro-poor spending as well as a framework to mobilize external resources, including those for pro-poor programs.

Many countries have also aimed at better targeting of social benefits to the most vulnerable. Since LICs often do not have well-targeted social benefit programs, the design and implementation of Fund-supported programs often involve close collaboration with the World Bank and regional development banks to increase the effectiveness of existing social programs. In the case of Mongolia, for instance, in addition to increasing overall social spending, the authorities are cooperating with the Asian Development Bank and the World Bank to undertake a study of the existing social benefits system, with a view to laying out policies for directing more resources to the poorest. More generally, in reflecting diverse circumstances, countries have applied varying approaches to achieving their goals of protecting the poor (see Box 3.4).

The External Counterpart to Policy Easing

Crisis programs have typically accommodated widening current account deficits, as a counterpart to fiscal easing (Figure 3.10). During the food and fuel price crisis of 2007–08, the expanded deficits were driven principally by terms-of-trade shocks; in 2009, a slump in export demand brought about by the global financial crisis was the overriding factor. With capital flows also retreating, programs since 2008 have generally incorporated drawdowns of official reserves to help finance the widening external deficits and limit import compression (Figure 3.11).

Increased IMF financing, by easing the external constraint, has played an important role in creating policy space for LICs in the face of the crises. For the sample of "continuous PRGF users" (see Box 3.2) on which this section is based, disbursements of concessional resources by the Fund doubled on average in 2008, relative both to the countries' quotas and to their GDP (Figure 3.12). This was made possible by larger initial loan amounts for new programs and, in some cases, additional resources at the time of program reviews. As of end-July 2009, average disbursements so far this year have already reached about 75 percent of the 2008 level, in part reflecting the doubling of access limits for the PRGF and ESF in April. A step-up in donor aid flows in 2008 also provided much-needed support for LIC budgets and balance of payments positions (see IMF, 2009e). As indicated earlier (in Box 3.1), however, LICs continue to face large external financing needs. Additional highly concessional donor support will be critical to help countries maintain an accommodating policy stance until economic activity rebounds, while avoiding unsustainable debt accumulation.

Figure 3.10. Current Account Deficit
(In percent of GDP)

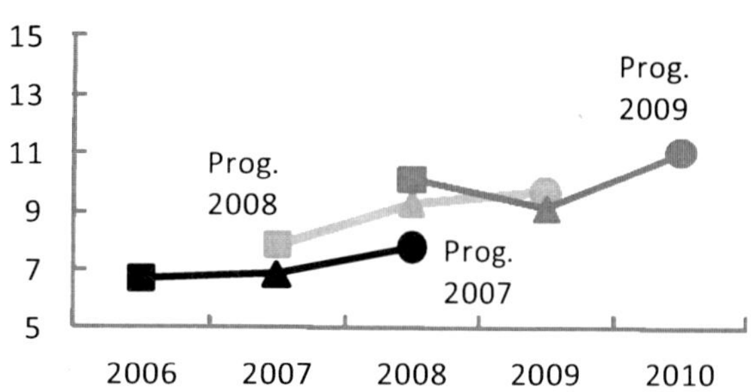

Source: Authors' estimates based on IMF staff reports.
■: Actual ▲: Projection for the year of program design
●: Program projection for the following year.

Figure 3.11. Gross Reserves[1]
(In percent of GDP)

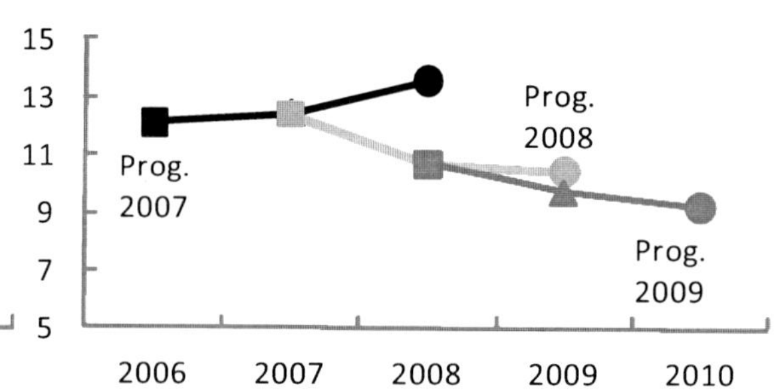

Source: Authors' estimates based on IMF staff reports.
■: Actual ▲: Projection for the year of program design
●: Program projection for the following year.
[1]Excludes Afghanistan and Grenada.

Figure 3.12. Average IMF Disbursements[1]

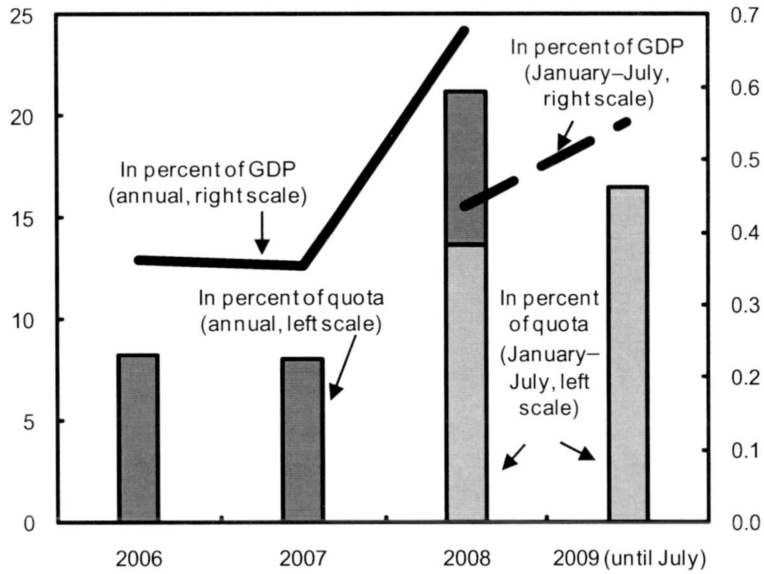

Source: Authors' estimates based on IMF staff reports.

[1]Lighter columns and dashed line refer to the period January–July only.

CHAPTER

4 Streamlining Structural Conditionality

Policy Evolution

The 1980s saw increased use of structural conditionality in Fund-supported programs. This was motivated by the view that structural reforms were essential to sustain macroeconomic adjustment and to create a needed environment for faster economic growth and poverty reduction. Amid weak growth performance and continued macroeconomic instability in the 1980s and 1990s in many LICs, the Fund came under heavy attack for its approach to structural conditionality. Critics, led by CSOs but also including many other stakeholders, disputed that structural reforms advocated by the Fund really promote growth and macroeconomic stability. Moreover, structural conditionality was seen as burdensome and often intrusive, thus undermining national ownership of reforms and overwhelming local capacity to implement them. This criticism intensified in the aftermath of the Asian financial crisis of 1997–98, during which many considered that structural conditionality in Fund-supported programs was too expansive and unhelpful for resolving the crisis. In short, critics were concerned that the Fund had lost its focus and strayed into areas where it had little expertise.[1]

In a streamlining initiative launched in 2000, the Fund confirmed the role of structural reforms in macroeconomic adjustment but emphasized the principle of parsimony for conditionality. This principle was subsequently reflected in new Conditionality Guidelines, which required that program-related conditions be "applied parsimoniously," stipulating that structural conditions must be "critical for the achievement of program goals" (see IMF, 2002b). For LICs, this meant that structural reforms—however beneficial they may be from a broader perspective—should be subject to conditionality only if they are critical to the achievement of macroeconomic stability that is consistent with sustained growth and poverty reduction.

---

[1]See Independent Evaluation Office (IEO) (2007) for a useful survey of these criticisms. Boxes 1 and 2 in the main IEO report provide succinct summaries.

A 2007 evaluation of Fund structural conditionality by the Fund's Independent Evaluation Office (IEO) became an impetus for further reform (IEO, 2007). The evaluation found that while the streamlining initiative indeed helped shift the composition of conditionality toward the core areas of the Fund's responsibility (namely, macroeconomic stabilization) and new areas of basic reforms (e.g., the financial sector), it did not reduce the volume of conditionality, and some conditions were not critical for the achievement of program goals.[2] In response, in March 2008, Fund management introduced an implementation plan aimed at further sharpening the application of the 2002 Conditionality Guidelines by requiring better justification of macrocriticality, establishing explicit links between goals, strategies and conditionality, and improving program documentation.

Earlier in 2009, the Fund introduced a new framework for applying structural conditionality. Under the new policy, progress in structural reforms that are critical for achieving the objectives of the Fund-supported programs will be monitored and assessed through reviews by the Fund's Executive Board. Use of structural performance criteria was discontinued on May 1, 2009 in all Fund-supported programs, including those for LICs, and specific structural conditions that are monitored under reviews will take the form of structural benchmarks. The aim is to provide countries with more flexibility in achieving their reform goals, putting more focus on the goals themselves and less on specific time-bound measures, thereby enhancing ownership and the likelihood of improving results. Because the new review-based conditionality will rely on selected structural benchmarks, however, the need for parsimony and criticality in defining those benchmarks remains.

Changing Practice

To assess whether recent LIC programs have indeed become more focused in the use of structural conditionality, we look at trends since the beginning of this decade. The analysis covers structural conditions in three types of programs with LICs (under the PRGF, Policy Support Instruments [PSIs], and Stand-By Arrangements [SBAs]) approved from January 2001 to June 2009.[3] Recent crisis-related programs (2008–09) are compared with those during 2001–04 (which were covered in the 2007 IEO evaluation of structural conditionality) and 2005–07 (the post-evaluation period).

[2]This confirmed the finding of a 2005 review by the IMF's Executive Board on the application of the 2002 Conditionality Guidelines. The review found that conditionality had shifted away from areas in which the Fund is not specialized. See IMF (2005b, 2005c).

[3]Since the Rapid-Access Component of the ESF does not involve conditionality, it is not covered in this paper. Most ESF-HAC programs either had no structural conditionality or had conditionality tied to concurrent PSI programs and are thus not counted separately in this analysis. The analysis covers 68 programs in 46 LICs.

Figure 4.1. Average Number of Conditions per Review

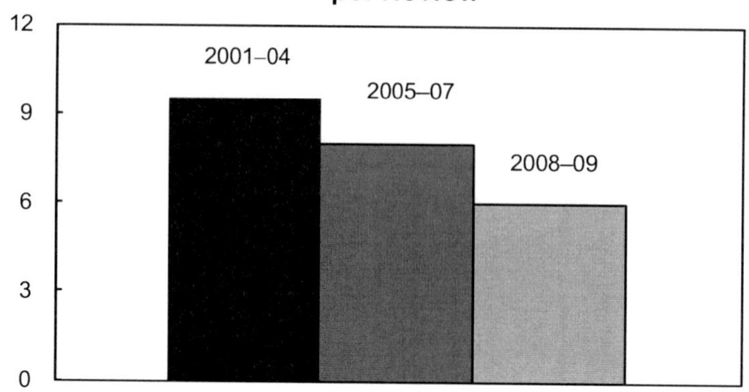

Sources: MONA database; and authors' estimates.

The number of conditions per program review has been declining since 2001–04.[4] By 2008–09, the average had fallen to six conditions per review, compared with nine per review during 2001–04, the last period covered by the 2007 IEO evaluation (Figure 4.1).[5] About one-third of programs initiated during 2008–09 had five conditions per review or less, whereas during 2001–04 fewer than one program in ten fell below that threshold (Figure 4.2).

The average number of conditions shows some variation across program and condition types. PRGF-supported programs have tended to have more conditions than other types of programs (Figure 4.3), but have shared in the generally declining trend (Figure 4.4).[6]

[4]Structural conditions include prior actions, structural performance criteria (or structural assessment criteria in the case of PSIs), and structural benchmarks. For a given program, the average number of structural conditions per review is calculated as the total number of conditions divided by the total number of reviews. The total number of reviews includes both completed reviews and (except when assessing the implementation rate) the next upcoming review. All results presented below are robust to the exclusion of SBAs. The analysis uses the same underlying data as the IEO 2007 evaluation, but a new data classification is used in this analysis, which gives a sharper focus on areas that are more likely to be critical to achieving program goals (see Annex 4).

[5]The average of nine conditions per program review reported here for the period 2001–04 is broadly consistent with the 17 conditions per program year reported by the IEO (2007), given that reviews are typically semiannual.

[6]An intertemporal comparison is made only for PRGF programs as the limited sample size of PSIs and SBAs renders it difficult to make such a comparison.

Figure 4.2. Distribution of Programs

(By number of conditions per review, in percent)

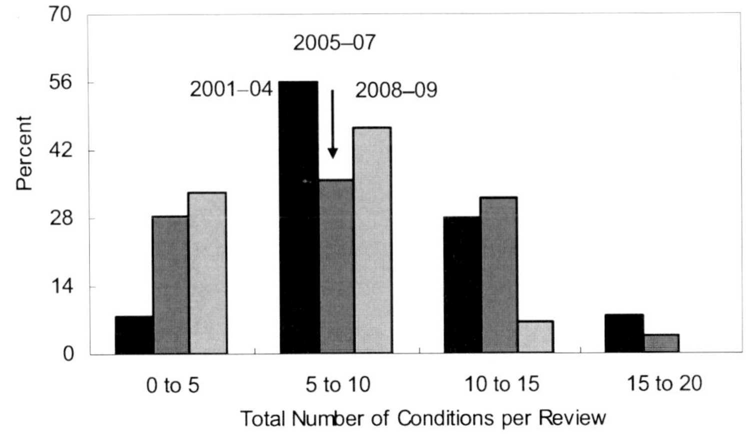

Sources: MONA database; and authors' estimates.

Figure 4.3. Average Number of Conditions per Review by Types of Programs and Conditions, 2001–09[1]

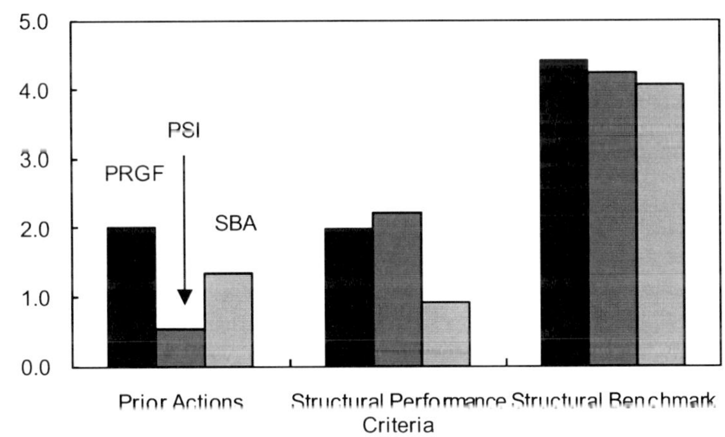

Sources: MONA database; and authors' estimates.

[1]PSI programs have structural assessment criteria in place of structural performance criteria.

Figure 4.4. Average Number of Conditions per PRGF Review
***(By type of conditions over time)*[1]**

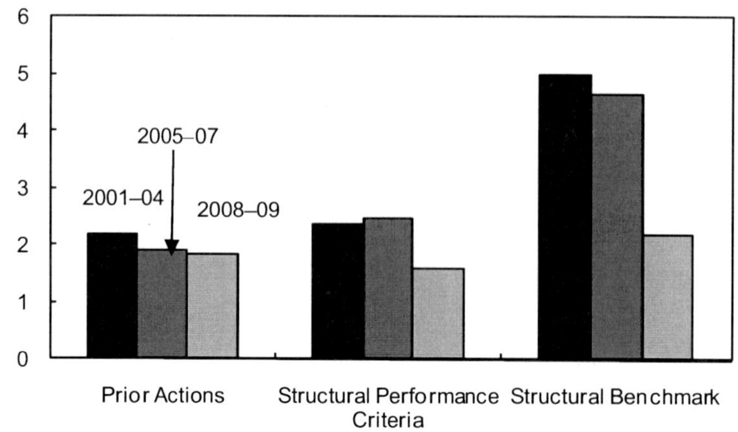

Sources: MONA database; and authors' estimates.
[1]PSI programs have structural assessment criteria in place of structural performance criteria.

Despite some redistribution over time, a key and consistent focus of structural conditionality has been measures related to public sector resource management and accountability. This category of reforms is often critical to achieving program goals and is a major area of Fund specialization, as part of its shared responsibilities with the World Bank. It is by far the most widely featured category in LIC program conditionality (Figure 4.5; see Annex 4 for the types of reform that come under this heading) and also an area where most stakeholders, including donors and CSOs, agree that conditionality is important and appropriate.[7] Box 4.1 illustrates how program conditionality in Liberia and Senegal has focused on this area, along with fiscal policy and other measures needed to achieve program objectives.

The use of structural conditionality has responded to the increasing need to mitigate pressure on public finances during the global crises. Huge increases in world oil prices during 2007–08 placed substantial strains on budget

[7]For instance, in suggesting how IMF gold sales could be used, Jubilee USA Network (2009, p. 2) notes that "The most efficient and practical way to deliver these resources is by providing IMF and multilateral debt service relief for eligible HIPCs and other low-income countries that have effective and transparent public financial management practices." Similarly, Pretorius and Pretorius (2009, p. 5) note that "Strong Public Financial Management (PFM) systems are essential to improved service delivery, poverty reduction and to achievement of the MDGs. Effective PFM systems maximise financial efficiency, improve transparency and accountability, and—in theory—will contribute to long-term economic success."

Figure 4.5. Distribution of Structural Conditions per Review
(In percent)

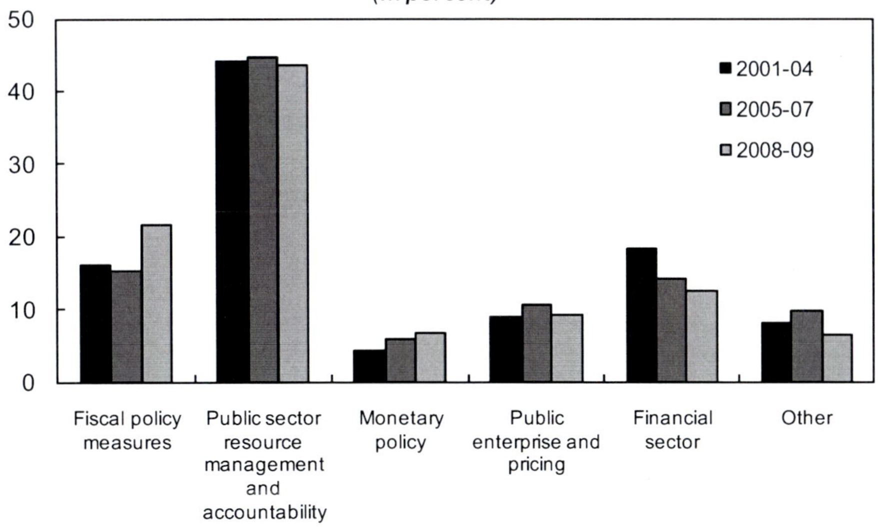

Sources: MONA Database; and authors' estimates.

outlays in countries where governments sought to mitigate the price impact by reducing taxes, providing subsidies and/or preventing domestic prices from adjusting fully. Similarly, the global financial crisis has adversely affected revenue collections while increasing the need for higher spending to support economic activity and protect the poor. Consequently, programs initiated in 2008–09 have exhibited a significant increase in conditionality on fiscal policy measures to address such problems. Specific measures in the fiscal area were often related to mitigating the impact of rising food and energy prices on the poor, such as adopting temporary subsidies on products most vital for the poor, eliminating or reducing import tariffs on key food and energy products, and expanding school feeding programs. Other measures often sought to control the impact of the price increases on government budgets, by liberalizing domestic fuel prices, adjusting electricity tariffs, and repatriating oil proceeds to governments.

With more parsimonious conditionality there has been an increase in the implementation rate of reforms. Since 2001–04, the proportion of conditions met has increased by 15 percentage points, to 86 percent (Figures 4.6 and 4.7).[8] The improvement in the implementation rate during 2008–09 is especially notable, given the likelihood that more challenging structural

[8]This result is robust to the exclusion of prior actions as well as SBAs and PSIs.

Figure 4.6. Average Share of Total Conditions Met
(In percent)

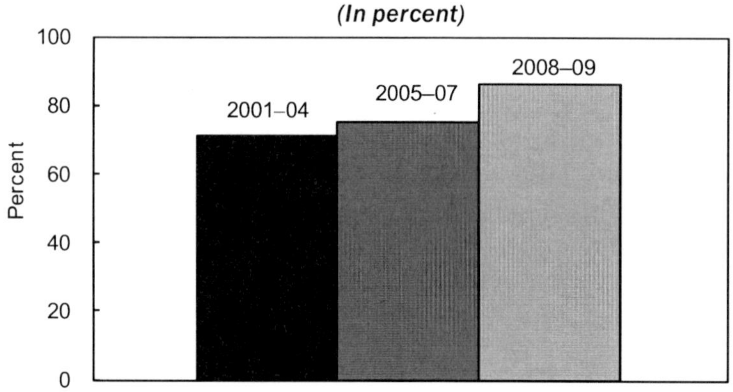

Sources: MONA database; and authors' estimates.

Figure 4.7. Average Share of Conditions Met by Type of Conditionality
(In percent)

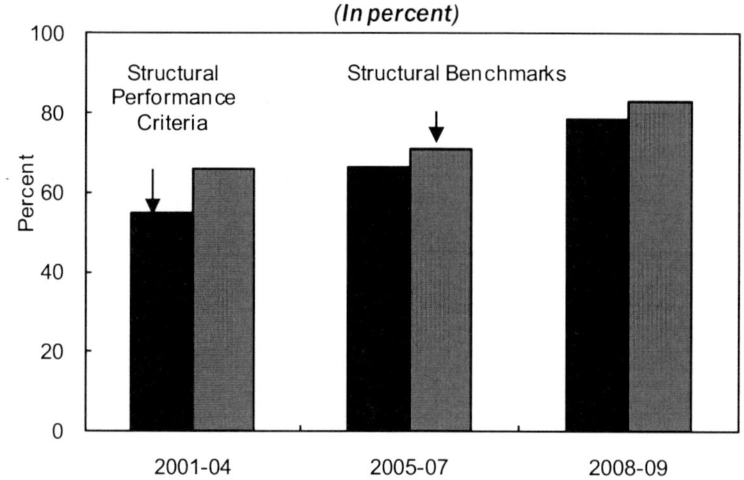

Sources: MONA database; and authors' estimates.

reforms may have been required to deal with the impact of the global crises. Although the likelihood of implementing a reform is influenced by many factors, more parsimonious conditionality should in principle lessen administrative burdens on implementation and help country authorities focus on their reform priorities. This should also bode well for country ownership of reforms.

Box 4.1. Structural Conditionality in Liberia and Senegal

Liberia

The main goal of Liberia's current three-year PRGF-Extended Fund Facility (EFF) supported program, which was initiated in March 2008 and provides critical support for the country's Heavily Indebted Poor Country (HIPC) debt relief process, is to sustain economic reconstruction in the postconflict era. The program is designed to create a stable macroeconomic environment to underpin rapid economic growth, job creation, poverty reduction, and progress toward the Millennium Development Goals (MDGs). The program centers on reinforcing economic governance, especially PFM and anticorruption efforts.

In supporting the program objectives, structural conditionality focuses on strengthening public institutions. Seven out of the 13 structural conditions set for the first year of the program were targeted at legislation and other actions to strengthen fiscal institutions and transparency. Two further conditions were aimed at improving regulatory oversight of the banking sector by instituting a regular program of bank inspections and at resolving the status of abandoned and nonoperating banks. These measures were critical steps to revive Liberia's banking sector. Other conditions are related to the development of strategies for debt management, civil service reforms, and national statistical development and to the establishment of a functioning anticorruption commission, a critical institution for implementing the country's anticorruption strategy.

As structural reforms have proceeded, conditionality has been streamlined but has remained focused on the program objectives. The number of conditions was reduced from 12 to 8 for the first and second reviews, and all performance criteria with a target date after May 1, 2009 were converted into structural benchmarks. As the legislative foundation for fiscal institutions was being laid, conditions began to target more specific measures in the areas of PFM, including issuance of PFM regulations, auditing of the central government accounts and promulgating regulations and guidelines under the Public Procurement and Concessions Act. In the financial sector, after establishing a system of off site inspections, a condition was set on completing on-site inspection reports for commercial banks to reinforce the soundness and stability of the banking system. The Fund has provided substantial technical assistance in helping the Liberian authorities strengthen their capacity to implement these reforms.

Senegal

Senegal's PSI program, initiated in late 2007, was aimed at returning the economy to a sustainable path and increasing its growth potential. To achieve this goal, a key focus of the program was to restore prudent fiscal policy to support macroeconomic stability and to raise public sector effectiveness by improving fiscal governance and transparency.

With this focus in mind, structural conditionality has emphasized reforms in public sector accountability and financial management as well as fiscal measures. Since the initiation of the program, with three subsequent reviews, two-thirds of structural conditionality has been in the area of public sector accountability and financial management. Adding fiscal policy measures, over 80 percent of structural conditionality revolves around fiscal policy and public sector accountability and financial management. Over time, the number of conditions was reduced from 12 for the first review to 7 for the fourth review.

Box 4.1 ***(concluded)***

The program was designed to progressively deepen macrocritical structural reforms. Prior to the PSI engagement, the authorities had identified public sector accountability and financial management measures as a priority for reform. In fact, they had developed a PFM action plan in conjunction with donors. The initial public sector accountability measures drew on this agenda, and each subsequent program review made adaptations to achieve progressive results. In the area of improving fiscal accounts, for instance, the initial program began with a structural benchmark on forwarding the government's end-year Treasury accounts for past years to the Audit Office. In the following review, a structural benchmark was set to resolve auditing payment delays. This was followed by very specific measures aimed at improving the reliability of budget monitoring systems and accurate assessments of expenditure carryovers from one year to the next. Most recently, a structural benchmark has been set on auditing the budget monitoring system, which is expected to improve its efficiency and expand the coverage of budget operations.

CHAPTER

5 Conclusions

Over the past decade, since the advent of the PRGF, the Fund has sought to refocus its programs with LIC members. Macroeconomic policies, though still geared toward ensuring sustainability, were intended to become more supportive of growth and poverty reduction objectives, including by safeguarding social and other critical spending in times of adjustment. Structural reforms were viewed as essential to underpin macroeconomic stability, growth and poverty reduction, but only measures critical to achieving those goals should be the subject of program conditionality.

The global food, fuel and financial crises have put to the test the Fund's ability to adhere to these principles, while responding quickly and creatively to LICs' rapidly changing needs. The revamp of lending facilities and scaling up of financial assistance, coupled with a new conditionality framework, represented an unprecedented effort by the Fund to help its low-income members. But questions continued to be raised as to whether the Fund was ready to adapt its macroeconomic policy advice to give LICs the room for maneuver they needed to tackle the multiple shocks, and to continue streamlining conditionality even in a context of new or intensified policy challenges.

The evidence presented in this paper indicates that, indeed, LICs' recent Fund-supported programs have been adapted to provide considerable space for countercyclical policies. In 2007–08, inflation targets were revised upward to accommodate the first-round effects of soaring world food and fuel prices. As these prices fell in the second half of 2008, targets were revised downward gradually to allow monetary policy to continue supporting economic activity and to achieve a gradual transition to a low-inflation environment. Fiscal policies were generally relaxed, to accommodate the social protection and other costs associated with the price shocks. Subsequently, as the global downturn hit, programs provided for further fiscal easing, not only by allowing automatic stabilizers to work on the revenue side, but also in many cases through increased spending. Countries were encouraged to safeguard and, in most instances, expand social protection and other core spending, targeted toward the most vulnerable. Consistent with the Fund's general policy advice to its members, countries with more vulnerable debt positions adopted a relatively cautious fiscal stance, but even their programs typically provided for widening fiscal deficits in 2009.

Past gains in macroeconomic stabilization, including reduced public debt and strengthened fiscal and external positions, helped create the needed space for countercyclical policy during the twin crises. Countries have been able to tap domestic financing sources as well as draw on accumulated official reserves. Many have sought new or expanded access to Fund loans to moderate reserve losses and ease financing constraints. Rising aid flows in 2008 also provided much-needed additional support.

The steady progress in recent years toward more streamlined structural conditionality continued under the LICs' crisis-response programs. The average number of conditions per review has declined by one-third since 2001–04—the final period covered by the IEO review of structural conditionality, which called for greater parsimony. The dominant focus of conditionality in LIC programs continues to be public sector resource management and accountability, an area where there is broad consensus among stakeholders, including many critics of the Fund, on the need for close monitoring. The rate of implementation of reforms has continued to increase as conditionality has become more parsimonious. More selective conditionality should enhance ownership of programs, as it enables country authorities to leverage their limited administrative resources for implementing priority reforms.

Looking ahead, countries will need to be ready to adapt their policies again as the impact of the global recession unwinds. Expenditures that were intended to provide temporary support to the economy will likely need to be scaled back, and fiscal deficits should be reduced as revenues recover. Strong support from donors will be essential to ensure that countries are not forced to make these adjustments prematurely, and to underpin macroeconomic policies that will ensure debt sustainability and promote long-term growth. Further improvements in revenue administration, public financial management and debt management are needed to mobilize more resources and use them more efficiently.

ANNEX

1 Analysis of Macroeconomic Policy Design Using WEO Data

The purpose of this analysis is to show whether the findings obtained for continuous PRGF programs in the main text broadly apply to all programs in LICs. The WEO dataset used covers all 37 program LICs as of end-July 2009 (see Annex 2 for the country list).[26] These countries are divided into two groups—those that initiated their programs before 2008 and those during 2008–09.[27] This distinction helps gauge the extent to which the difference in the nature of programs and the timing of their initiation could influence their objectives. Pre-2008 programs consist of PRGFs and PSIs which are aimed at resolving protracted balance of payments problems. Post-2008 programs include—in addition to PRGFs and PSIs—SBAs and ESFs that are designed to address short-term balance of payments problems. Post-2008 programs were designed in the midst of the twin global crises and were more likely than pre-2008 programs to have taken into account the need to address the impact of the crises. Pre-2008 programs, on the other hand, will more likely need to be modified in subsequent reviews to address the consequence of the crises.

As the impact of the food, fuel and global financial crises was increasingly being felt, programs began to factor in a significant growth slowdown. The October 2007 WEO projected steady growth in 2008–10 for both pre- and post-2008 program countries (Figure A1). As the global economic outlook deteriorated with the onset of the global financial crisis, the October 2008 WEO revised growth projections downward, more so for post-2008 program

[26]The database includes observations on macrovariables from October 2007, October 2008, and April 2009 WEO revisions covering the period 2006–10. Each WEO vintage includes different actual and projection periods. For example, October 2007 WEO observations include actual observations for 2006 and projections for 2007–10. As actual data become available in subsequent WEO revisions, both actual observations and projections are updated. Thus, the April 2009 WEO revision includes actual observations for 2006–08 and projections for 2009–10 (and beyond).

[27]Hereafter, the former group is referred to as pre-2008 program countries and the latter group as post-2008 program countries.

Figure A1. Real GDP Growth, Inflation, and Change in Broad Money
(In percent)

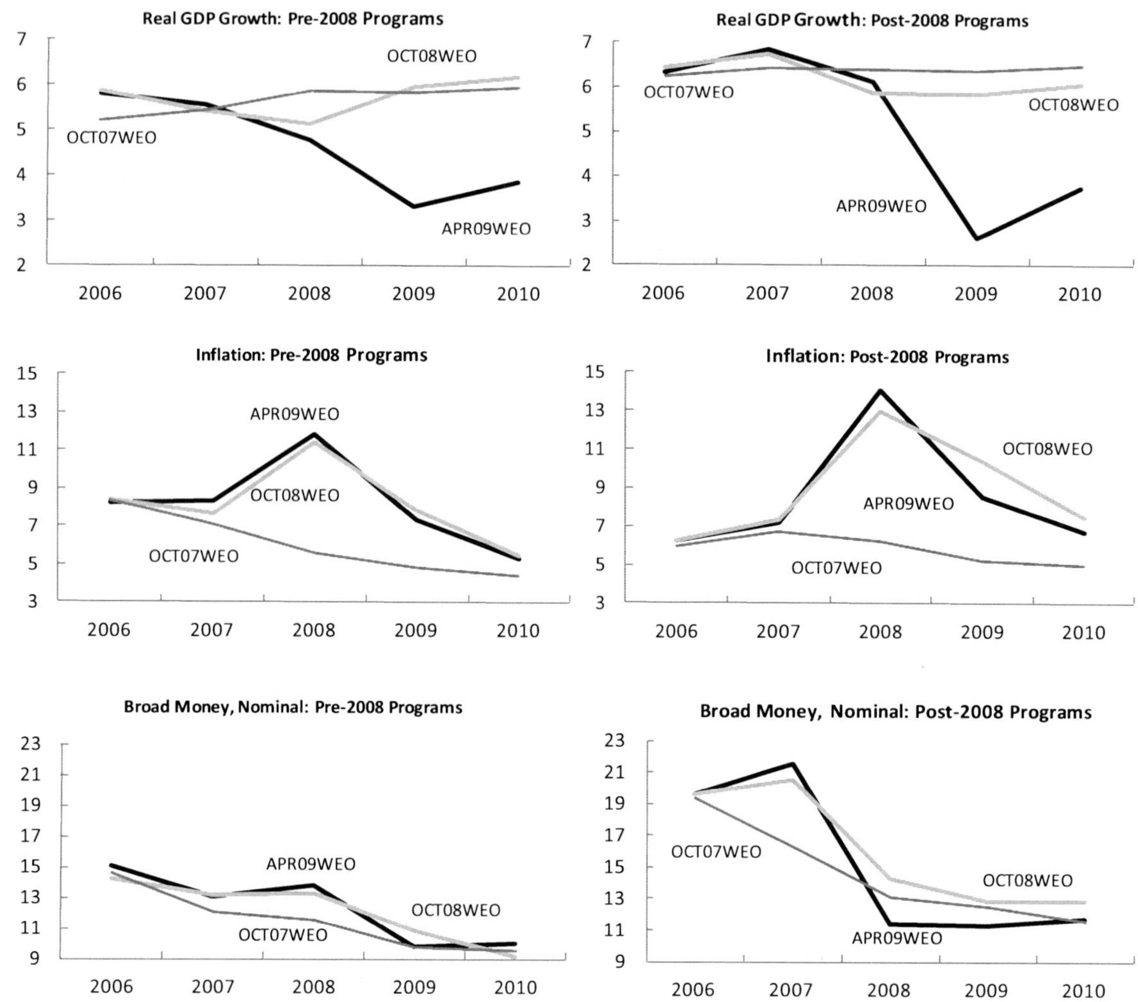

Sources: WEO database; and IMF staff estimates.

countries than for pre-2008 program countries. By the time of the April 2009 WEO revision, projected growth was revised down by about 3 percentage points for 2009 and 2 percentage points for 2010, for both groups of countries.

Inflation objectives and monetary policy have been adjusted to accommodate the first-round effect of increasing world food and fuel prices. As food and fuel prices rose, monetary policy was eased and inflation projections for both groups of countries were revised significantly upwards in October 2008 (Figure A1). As food and fuel prices began to fall in mid-2008 and money demand weakened with slowing economic activity in the wake of the global financial crisis, money supply was adjusted downward for 2009 to prevent the second-round effects of the price increases. Despite the adjustment, however, inflation in both groups of countries is expected to come down only gradually to allow monetary policy to support short-term economic activity in the face of an economic downturn.

Fiscal policy was loosened in response to a deteriorating economic outlook. In pre-2008 program countries, 2007 and 2008 projections envisaged a large increase in the primary deficit in 2008 but a consolidation in 2009. As the impact of the global financial crisis became more evident in 2009, projections envisaged a continued deterioration of the fiscal balance in 2009, with a projected improvement only in 2010. In post-2008 program countries, the October 2007 WEO projected a sharp deterioration in the primary balance for 2007 (partly reflecting the one-off effect of debt relief under the Multilateral Debt Relief Initiative in 2006), followed by a stable outlook. Subsequent WEO revisions projected some further increase in the deficit in 2008 and similar levels of deficits in 2009. This outlook reflected a policy to allow automatic stabilizers to work on the revenue side and to increase expenditures at the same time. A similar policy appears to have been at work in pre-2008 countries (Figure A2).

In relaxing fiscal stances debt vulnerabilities have been taken into account.[28] Primary fiscal balances in pre-2008 program countries with low and moderate risks of debt distress were projected to deteriorate during the period 2006–10. In contrast, primary fiscal balances in countries with high debt distress risk were projected to remain stable throughout the period. The pattern is similar for post-2008 program countries, except that countries with low debt distress risks started with a stronger fiscal position and were projected to loosen their fiscal stance even more than their pre-2008 counterparts. Debt dynamics also reflect a more accommodating fiscal stance in countries with low and moderate debt distress risks. The debt-to-GDP ratio was projected to increase for countries with low and moderate debt distress risks, while remaining stable for countries with high debt distress risks (Figure A3).

Program countries have been able to smooth external account adjustment by slowing reserve buildup and adjustment patterns have reflected debt vulnerabilities. Both groups of countries were projected to experience a sharp deterioration in their current account balances in 2007–08 as a result of rising world food and fuel prices. The deterioration turned out to be larger than projected for both groups, but more so in post-2008 program countries,

[28]Debt distress ratings reflect the latest DSA assessments as of end-July 2009.

Figure A2. Primary Balance, Revenues, and Expenditures
(In percent of GDP)

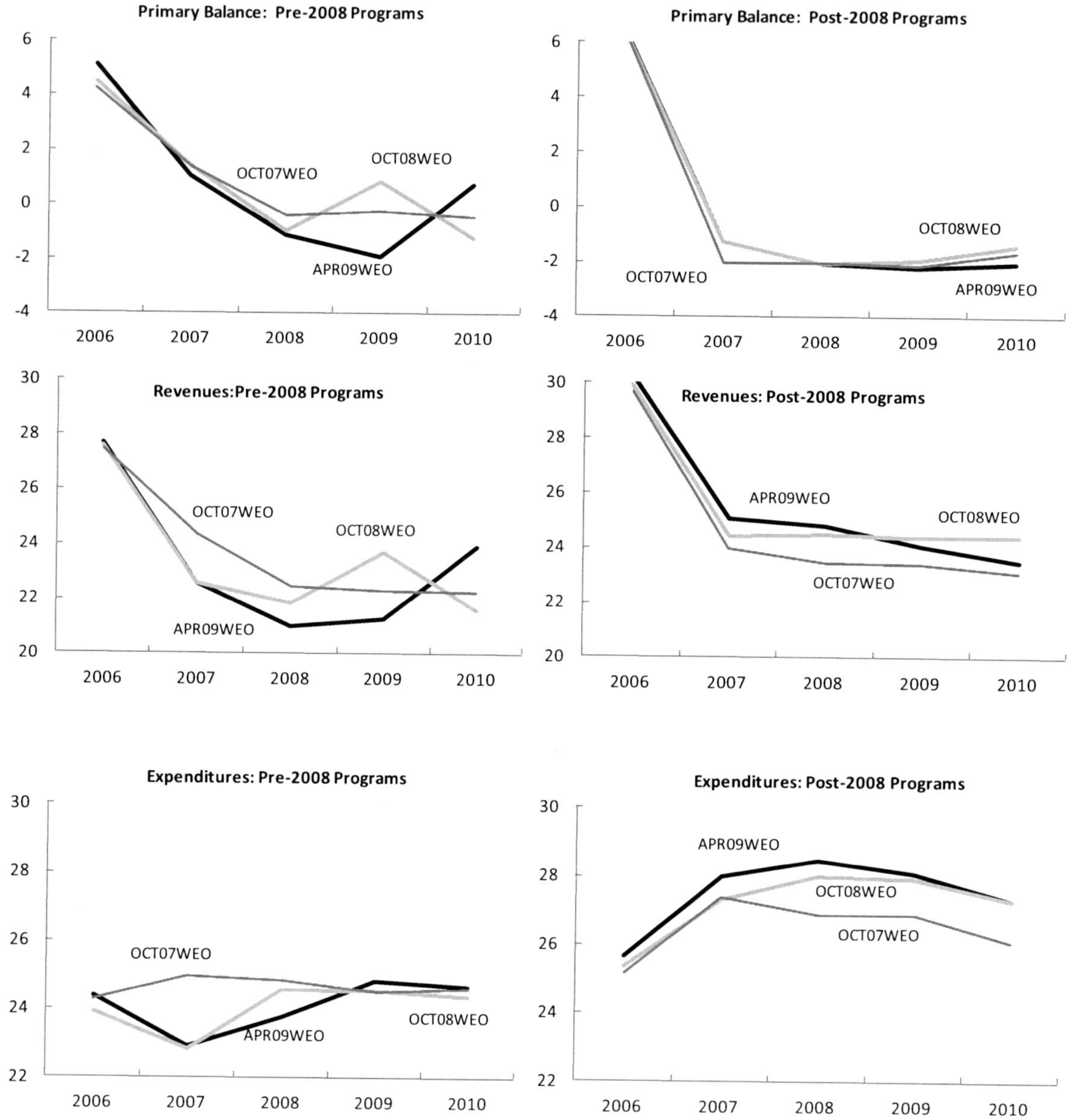

Sources: WEO database; and IMF staff estimates.

Figure A3. Outstanding Debt and Primary Balance by Debt Vulnerabilities
(In percent of GDP)

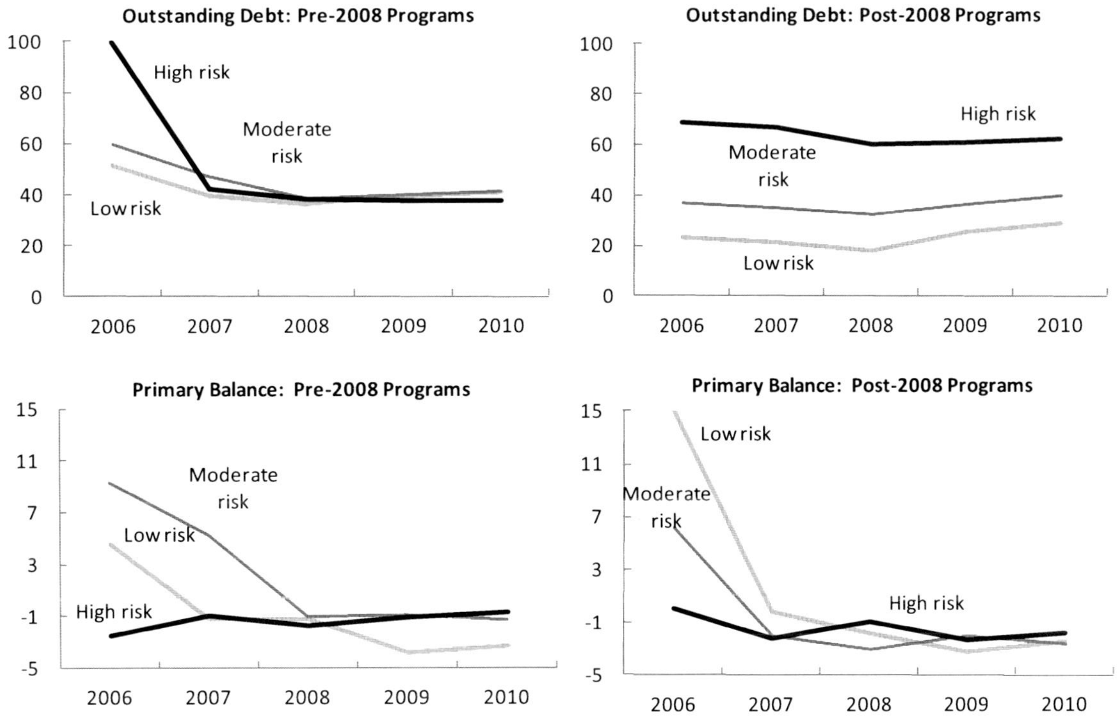

Sources: WEO database; and IMF staff estimates.

which were able to use their higher level of initial reserves to finance a larger increase in the current account deficit. Countries with lower and moderate debt distress risks entered the crises with higher reserve coverage and considerably lower current account deficits. As a result, they were able to finance a larger increase in the current account deficit in 2007 and 2008, and undertake slower adjustment in 2009 and 2010 (Figure A4).

Figure A4. Current Account Deficit in Percent of GDP, and Reserves in Months of Imports

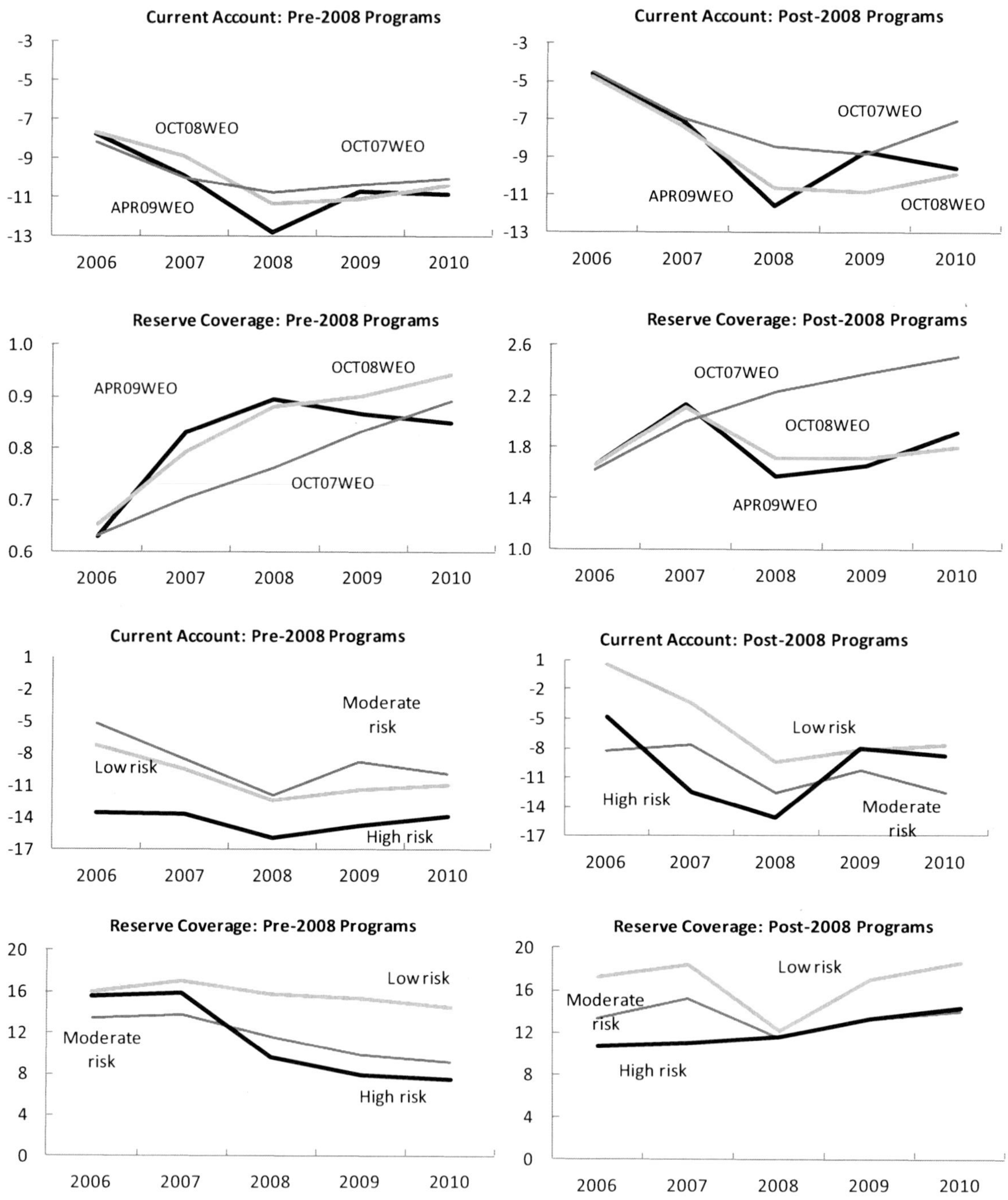

Sources: WEO database; and IMF staff estimates.

ANNEX

2 List of Countries with Program Engagements

Program start date in 2002–04		Program start date in 2005–07		Program start date in 2008–09			Program start date in 2005–07 and active in 2008–09	
SBA	PRGF	PSI	PRGF	SBA	PRGF	ESF-HAC	PSI	PRGF
2 countries:	*21 countries:*	*6 countries:*	*21 countries:*	*5 countries:*	*12 countries:*	*2 countries:*	*5 countries:*	*13 countries:*
Bolivia	Albania	Cape Verde	Afghanistan	Armenia	Burundi	Kyrgyz Rep.	Cape Verde	Afghanistan
Dominica	Bangladesh	Mozambique	Albania	Georgia	Congo, Rep. of	Malawi	Mozambique	Benin
	Burkina Faso	Nigeria	Armenia	Mongolia	Côte d'Ivoire		Senegal	Burkina Faso
	Burundi	Senegal	Benin	Pakistan	Djibouti		Tanzania	Gambia, The
	Cape Verde	Tanzania	Burkina Faso	Sri Lanka	Ghana		Uganda	Grenada
	Congo, Rep. of	Uganda	Cameroon		Liberia			Guinea
	Dominica		Central African Republic		Mali			Haiti
	Georgia		Gambia, The		Niger			Madagascar
	Ghana		Grenada		São Tomé and Príncipe			Mauritania
	Honduras		Guinea		Tajikistan			Nicaragua
	Kenya		Haiti		Togo			Rwanda
	Mali		Kyrgyz Rep.		Zambia			Sierra Leone
	Mozambique		Madagascar					Central African Republic
	Nepal		Malawi					
	Nicaragua		Mauritania					
	Rwanda		Moldova					
	Senegal		Nicaragua					
	Tajikistan		Niger					
	Tanzania		Rwanda					
	Uganda		São Tomé and Príncipe					
	Zambia		Sierra Leone					

ANNEX

3 Social Issues: Program Measures in 2008–09

Armenia (SBA)	*Higher social spending.* The IMF-supported program includes an increase in social spending of 1.6 percent of GDP in 2009 compared to 2008.
Burundi (PRGF)	*Higher social spending.* The impact of higher food and oil prices on the poor is mitigated by enhancing social safety nets (e.g., food security programs and school feeding programs). To boost food production, the government distributed seeds and fertilizers to smallholders, provided microcredits, and rehabilitated irrigation systems. The budgetary costs of these measures (estimated at about 3 percent of GDP) was fully financed by donors.
Congo, Republic of (PRGF)	*Higher social spending and focus on pro-poor spending.* In collaboration with the World Bank, the program envisages quarterly monitoring of pro-poor spending.
Côte d'Ivoire (PRGF)	*Higher social spending and focus on improving social indicators.* In collaboration with the World Bank, the program envisages quarterly monitoring of pro-poor spending and progress on social indicators. HIPC Completion-Point triggers include safer childbirth, thereby protecting the lives of women and children, and greater access to textbooks to ensure quality education.
Djibouti (PRGF)	*Higher social spending and better targeting.* In collaboration with the World Bank, the program envisages biannual monitoring of pro-poor spending and progress on social indicators. Social concerns raised by increasing food and oil prices are addressed by developing a system of targeted subsidies to the poorest, with World Bank assistance.
Georgia (SBA)	*Higher social spending.* Social spending is projected to increase by one percent of GDP in 2009 compared to 2008. Fiscal policy is set to support economic activity while addressing key social and reconstruction needs. Recurrent spending (mainly on defense) is expected to fall sharply while social outlays increase.
Ghana (PRGF)	*Better targeting.* To mitigate the risks associated with slower growth for low-income and vulnerable groups, social protection and safety nets will be strengthened and expanded. Social protection programs, particularly in health, education and sanitation, will be preserved. New initiatives include the provision of school uniforms to about 1.6 million pupils in public basic schools in deprived communities. Free exercise books will also be provided for every pupil in all public basic schools. In addition, the current capitation grant will be increased by 50 percent.

The Kyrgyz Republic (ESF-HAC)	*Higher social spending.* Social fund expenditures are programmed to increase by 0.5 percent of GDP in 2009. The surge in food and fuel prices and growing energy supply difficulties prompted a rapid and coordinated response from the donor community. The World Bank, European Union, Asian Development Bank, European Bank for Reconstruction and Development, U.S. Agency for International Development, United Nations Food and Agriculture Organization, and other organizations are providing loans, grants and in-kind assistance to support the agricultural and energy sectors.
Liberia (PRGF)	*Higher social spending and focus on improving social indicators.* In collaboration with the World Bank, the program envisages quarterly monitoring of pro-poor spending and progress on social indicators.
Malawi (ESF-HAC)	*Higher social spending.* Higher revenues and aid and lower interest payments on public debt have allowed an increase in outlays for poverty-reducing and social expenditures.
Mali (PRGF)	*Higher social spending and better targeting.* The program supported the government's policy response to provide financial support to rice production through fertilizer and machinery subsidies; release food from village food banks; remove import taxes on limited quantities of rice, milk powder and cooking oil imports; and temporarily reduce taxation of petroleum products, particularly diesel. Costs of these measures, estimated at 1.8 percent of GDP in lost revenue, were accommodated in the program-supported budget framework. Looking ahead, in collaboration with the World Bank and the Fund, the government intends to evaluate experience and seek assistance in designing support programs targeted to the vulnerable and groups that are difficult to reach.
Mongolia (SBA)	*Higher social spending and improved targeting.* The program has a concrete timetable to better target social transfers in order to provide greater support to Mongolia's poorest citizens. In cooperation with the Asian Development Bank and the World Bank, the government will undertake a study of the existing social benefits system with a view to rationalizing untargeted social spending to direct more resources to the poorest.
Niger (PRGF)	*Higher social spending and focus on improving social indicators.* In collaboration with the World Bank, the program envisages quarterly monitoring of pro-poor spending and progress on social indicators.
Pakistan (SBA)	*Better targeting.* Strengthening social safety nets is a key priority under the IMF-supported program. Cash transfers to the poor are projected to increase from 0.4 percent of GDP in 2008–09 to 0.6 percent of GDP in 2009–10. The government is also collaborating with the World Bank to develop specific measures to strengthen social safety nets and improve targeting to the poor.
São Tomé and Príncipe (PRGF)	*Focus on improving social indicators.* In collaboration with the World Bank, the program envisages quarterly monitoring of pro-poor spending and progress on social indicators. Pro-poor Treasury-funded capital spending covers projects that are deemed to have a direct impact on alleviating poverty in the following sectors: education, health, social safety nets, agriculture and fisheries, rural development, youth and sports, provision of potable water, and electrification. The social sector has benefited from African Development Bank Group financing.

Sri Lanka (SBA)	*Higher social spending.* To protect the vulnerable, social sector spending is targeted to increase to 7 percent of GDP in 2009 from 6.8 percent in 2008. For the 2010 budget, the authorities are committed to achieving savings in military spending, which will create more space for social and reconstruction spending while allowing a further reduction in the budget deficit.
Tajikistan (PRGF)	*Higher social spending.* Fiscal policy will accommodate expected increases in demand for social spending. The revenue-to-GDP ratio is expected to decline by close to 2.8 percent of GDP in 2009. At the same time, the authorities intend to raise social spending on transfers to households, health and education by almost 1.5 percent of GDP, and they are working closely with the World Bank in these areas.
Togo (PRGF)	*Higher social spending.* The government intends to increase the share of priority spending on social and physical capital, in line with its PRS objectives. Priority spending is programmed to increase by 2.4 percent of GDP in 2009 and an additional 3 percent of GDP in 2010.
Zambia (PRGF)	*Higher social spending.* The fiscal deficit in 2009 is projected to widen in order to accommodate increased expenditure on infrastructure and social services, in line with the authorities' objectives of encouraging diversification and enhancing competitiveness.

ANNEX

4 A New Classification of Structural Conditionality

In reclassifying structural conditions, a key consideration is the likelihood that a condition is macrocritical and falls within the areas of core Fund expertise. A condition is of critical importance when program goals would not be achieved or program monitoring would not be possible without the implementation of the condition. In economic terms, such a condition is essential to addressing obstacles in correcting maladjustments in the balance of payments and safeguarding Fund resources. Although not all macrocritical conditions fall within the areas of Fund expertise, measures in these areas are more likely to be critical to achieving program goals. The areas of core Fund expertise are typically in the domain of macroeconomic stabilization—specifically, fiscal, monetary and exchange rate policies, including the underlying institutional arrangements and related structural measures, and financial systems issues related to the functioning of both domestic and international financial markets. Structural reforms that are aimed at strengthening public sector resource management and accountability are often central to building the foundation for macroeconomic stabilization. The new classification used in this study therefore highlights the intersection between macrocriticality and Fund expertise:

- *Fiscal policy measures* include measures that directly affect revenue by changing tax rates (other than taxes on international trade) or the tax base and measures that directly affect the amount of fiscal expenditures. They include revenue measures (excluding revenue administration and trade policy), combined expenditure and revenue measures, civil service and public employment reforms and wage policy, pension reforms, and other social sector reforms, including social safety net measures. They do not include budget preparation, submission and approval; intergovernmental relations; expenditure auditing; fiscal transparency and financial controls; and public expenditure management. These are included instead in the public sector resource management and accountability category.

- *Public sector resource management and accountability* comprises primarily public sector governance, transparency and financial management measures—including PFM measures. These include revenue administration (including customs administration); expenditure auditing, accounting, and financial controls; fiscal transparency (publication of public accounts and parliamentary oversight); budget preparation; and intergovernmental relations. Also included are central bank auditing, transparency and financial controls; PRSP development and implementation; and anticorruption legislation and policy.
- *Monetary policy, exchange rate policy and other central bank operations and reforms* cover monetary policy, measures related to the exchange system and exchange restrictions on current and capital account transactions, exchange rate policy, other central bank operations, and central bank reforms, but not central bank auditing, accounting and transparency, which are included in the public sector resource management and accountability category.
- *Public enterprise and pricing* includes public enterprise pricing and subsidies, privatization and steps toward privatization (except for the financial sector), and public enterprise reform and restructuring.
- *Financial sector reforms* consist of all measures related to the financial sector, apart from central bank operations, central bank auditing, accounting and transparency. The latter three areas are included in the public sector resource management and accountability category.
- *Other measures* include all other structural measures not included elsewhere. Specifically, they include policy on international trade (other than customs administration measures), labor market measures (other than those related to public sector employment), economic statistics (excluding reporting related to fiscal or central bank transparency and accountability), private sector legal and regulatory reform, and natural resource and agricultural policies (other than pricing and marketing measures).

References

Berg, Andres, Norbert Funke, Alejandro Hajdengerg, Victor Lledo, Rolando Ossowski, Martin Schindler, Antonio Spilimbergo, Shamsuddin Tareq, and Irene Yackovlev, 2009, "Fiscal Policy in Sub-Saharan Africa in Response to the Impact of the Global Crisis," IMF Staff Position Note 09/10 (Washington: International Monetary Fund).

Berndt, Marcus, Paolo Dudine, Jan Kees Martijn, and Abu Shonchoy, 2008, "The Spending and Absorption of Aid in PRGF Supported Programs," IMF Working Paper 08/237 (Washington: International Monetary Fund).

Eurodad, 2009, "Bail-Out or Blow-Out? IMF Policy Advice and Conditions for Low-Income Countries at a Time of Crisis," available at www.eurodad.org/uploadedFiles/Whats_New/Reports/Bail-out%20or%20blow-out.pdf.

Ghosh, Atish, Charis Christofides, Jun Kim, Laura Papi, Uma Ramakrishnan, Alun Thomas, and Juan Zalduendo, 2005, *The Design of IMF-Supported Programs,* IMF Occasional Paper No. 241 (Washington: International Monetary Fund).

International Monetary Fund (IMF), 2002a, "Review of the Poverty Reduction and Growth Facility—Issues and Options" (Washington).

———, 2002b, "Guidelines on Conditionality," available at www.imf.org/external/np/pdr/cond/2002/eng/guid/092302.htm.

———, 2005a, "Review of PRGF Program Design—Overview," August 8 (Washington).

———, 2005b, "Review of the 2002 Conditionality Guidelines," March 3 (Washington).

———, 2005c, "Review of the 2002 Conditionality Guidelines—Selected Issues," March 4 (Washington).

———, 2009a, "A New Architecture of Facilities for Low-Income Countries," June 26 (Washington).

———, 2009b, "Review of Recent Crisis Programs," September 14 (Washington).

———, 2009c, "The Fund's Facilities and Financing Framework for Low-Income Countries," February 25 (Washington).

———, 2009d, "The Implications of the Global Financial Crisis for Low-Income Countries," March 3 (Washington).

———, 2009e, "The Implications of the Global Financial Crisis for Low-Income Countries—An Update," September 28 (Washington).

———, and World Bank, 1999a, "The Poverty Reduction and Growth Facility (PRGF)—Operational Issues," December 13 (Washington: International Monetary Fund).

———, 1999b, "Poverty Reduction Strategy Papers—Operational Issues," December 10 (Washington: International Monetary Fund).

Independent Evaluation Office of the IMF (IEO), 2007, *Structural Conditionality in IMF-Supported Programs*, IEO evaluation report (Washington: International Monetary Fund).

Jubilee USA Network, 2009, "Leveraging the IMF's Pots of Gold for the Benefit of Low-Income Countries," position paper, updated May 2009, available at http://docs.google.com/gview?a=v&q=cache:8SuAf99r2t8J:www.jubileeusa.org/fileadmin/user_upload/Resources/G20/Jubilee_USA_IMF_Gold_Sales_for_LICs_Position_Paper_UPDATED_051509.pdf+IMF+structural+condition+on+public+financial+management+and+accountability+beneficial&hl=en&gl=us.

Pretorius, Carole, and Nico Pretorius, 2009, *Review of Public Financial Management Reform Literature,* Evaluation Working Paper/Evaluation Report No. EV698 (London: Department for International Development).

Ratha, Dilip, Sanket Mohapatra, and Ani Silwal, 2009, *Migration and Development Brief No. 10* (Washington: World Bank).

Third World Network (TWN), 2009, "The IMF's Financial Crisis Loans: No Change in Conditionalities," March 11, available at www.twnside.org.sg/title2/par/IMF.Crisis.Loans-Overview.TWN.March.2009.doc.